Open Your G.I.F.T.S.

22 Lessons on Finding and Embracing Your Personal Power

Open YOUR G.I.F.T.S.

22 Lessons on Finding and Embracing Your Personal Power

PRESENTED BY

KIM COLES

purposely created
PUBLISHING

Open Your G.I.F.T.S.

Published by Purposely Created Publishing Group™

Copyright © 2017 Kim Coles

All rights reserved.

Printed in the United States of America

ISBN: 978-1-945558-61-0

Table of Contents

Foreword

I'm Reginald McKiver, the husband of Kim Coles. When asked to write the foreword of her latest project, I deemed it as an honor. A chance to eternally submit in writing words that would endure throughout the ages about the woman I love with all of my heart. To be able to amplify her mark through the expression of writing. I support her and every woman who will express their interpretation of G.I.F.T.S.

When I first met Kim, she expressed her interest in G.I.F.T.S. and how she and others would use it to transform the world. She wanted to affect change and, in doing so, wanted to open the door for others to be able to do the same. "Everyone has a gift," she stated, and went on to say, "Who are we? Or anyone, to say that your gift is not important, or would not be life changing for others?" Kim did not want to be defined as an actor and was in the process of reinventing herself to do what she was born to do: spread joy.

Open Your G.I.F.T.S. is a collection of personal stories of triumph through adversity, enlightenment, perseverance, and tenacity—written by women who have embraced their personal power—to bring us together by opening up their souls to help free yours! What I love is that it calls you, the reader, to participate through creating not just a brilliant read, but an experience. Some of these women I know personally, and can attest to their greatness and their desire to be heard in a way that helps others.

Opening your G.I.F.T.S. is a momentum, a movement for such a time as this. By one woman opening her G.I.F.T.S., she has created a way to transfer this gift to another woman, and to another, and now to you. This makes it an energy in which you now become a partaker. No longer are we prisoners and partakers of our own story; we are now free to share our story and to unify. There is power in expression, a power of releasing actions and words that once had you bound, only to discover that your hurt has a dual purpose. That once what could have been set up to destroy you, has now turned into a blessing to the nation. Through this book, may you discover your power, your career changer, and your destiny enhancer.

Let this book, this movement, run. Pass it along to a neighbor, a friend, a sister or brother—anyone who struggles with their G.I.F.T. May it be a blessing to you. It is my prayer that Kim, and the women of these experiences, cause a transformation in your life. Keep this book handy, follow its application, and keep it moving.

It is an honor and a privilege.

Reginald McKiver

Introduction:
Time to Open Your G.I.F.T.S. and Share Them with the World

By Kim Coles

Although you may know me as an actress and a comedian (woo woo woo!), I have always been inspired to stretch and grow beyond the stage and screen by empowering and inspiring others.

I will be completely transparent with you. I have been on a wonderful personal journey in the last couple of years to find more PURPOSE and PASSION. Of course, I have been blessed to have a very interesting, varied, and fulfilling showbiz career. And yes, there have been ups and downs, but I have managed to stay afloat and remain grateful even when work was scarce.

However, you know how you get that feeling that there may be MORE out there, or should I say more *in* there? Have you ever wondered if you are living up to your fullest human potential? This has nothing to do with WHAT we do for a living, but everything to do with WHO we are in our spirit and soul. So many of us think that we are what we do. It is true that some of us find great purpose in what we do. However, the best life alignment and balance happens when we are clear about who we are at our core, and that sets us up to just BE in the energy of our best lives at all times.

In my personal quest, I found that there indeed was more inside of me that I wanted to share. I realized that I could be using my gifts even more fully. When I say gifts, I mean those exceptional qualities that we each have inside of us. I wanted to reach beyond the acting, standup comedy, and the red carpet, which I do. And now…I'm inviting YOU to reach to find your best gifts! We all came here to do something amazing and I want to see you find your passion, live your purpose, and *shine*!

Several years ago, after my successful five-year run of the hit Fox TV show *Living Single* ended, I went through an incredibly difficult depression, which culminated in a loss of confidence, self-worth, and faith. It wasn't just that I was missing my TV show family, or that I was now unemployed with no new income coming in, or that I was without a man again. It was the perfect storm of all of the above, and I felt that I lost my mojo. But the truth is… I'm not sure that I really had ever worked to find my mojo—you know, that inner strength, essence, and magical gift that lives inside us and must be felt, experienced, and called forth so we can be our BEST selves.

I know now that I needed to go through my darkest hours to come out on the other side. For the record, my darkest hours included shopping myself into extreme debt (with bill collectors constantly calling my house), eating myself into a 30-pound weight gain (potato chips are a helluva drug), and accepting abusive relationships. The worst abuse/offense was what I was doing to myself. I was angry, disappointed, and tired, leading to me do the unthinkable.

I turned away from God.

Where was GOD and why was I being punished? All of this was intensified by my need to hide my truth, so that fans and family would not find out that I was broke and broken. I felt like a failure and a fraud, depressed and embarrassed and in fear of being found out.

I was also worried that the bill collectors who called my home would sell my info to the tabloids. Plus, I didn't know how I was gonna make a "comeback." The pain became so unbearable that I considered suicide. I just wanted the pain to stop, and ending my life seemed to be the easiest choice. I was going to "off" myself by driving my Jeep off of a cliff of the world famous Mulholland Drive. Dramatic. Fiery. Final. One little hairpin turn of the steering wheel to the left or right, and the pain would end. But would it really, I wondered.

The pain that I would've caused my wonderful parents is what stopped me. They didn't deserve that. With that simple truth and momentary return to my senses, I realized that only I could change my circumstances. The first step was getting myself in therapy. One of the first suggestions of that first step was starting a gratitude journal. I scoffed. *Gratitude? Doesn't this lady see how much pain that I am in?*

I was instructed to write down five things that I was grateful for every day. Within 30 days of journaling, I felt better and stronger. I learned that no matter your circumstances, seeking things to be grateful for creates more opportunities for joy and possibilities. Sometimes that's all you need. This exercise opened me and helped me in such a beautiful way that I felt the need to serve others by sharing the value I was finding by simply giving thanks.

That was the beginning of a beautiful journey.

The next step was my decision to become an evangelist for gratitude and sharing my truth. I thought to myself, I cannot be the only one in this pain, and if I share with others, maybe I can help. Along the way, I realized that we *all* have powerful gifts inside of us. Now, because I think that I'm sooo clever, I came up with an acronym for gifts. If we explore Gratitude Intention Forgiveness Triumphs, and Self-love, we can open the gifts that are inside of us, share them with others, and enjoy a more fulfilled life and mojo!

GRATITUDE

When you start your day in a place of gratitude, you are setting yourself up to win! No matter what your life looks like at this moment, there is certainly something to be grateful for and you get to fill your heart with anything and everything for which you feel appreciation. And just you wait, more is coming too!

INTENTION

"Our intention creates our reality." -Wayne Dyer

This powerful concept is all around us. It is about staying "on purpose" and living with deliberateness. Your intentions will help you to take greater control of your life. If you have a purpose or plan in mind, then you have direction and a better chance of success in the area you are focusing on. I call intention my "spiritual to-do list."

Invitation of Intention: Write five intentions that speak to your spirit each day. Only write the ones that you will remain dedicated and motivated to do.

FORGIVENESS

"He who has injured thee was stronger or weaker than thee. If weaker, spare him; if stronger, spare thyself." -Roman Stoic philosopher, Seneca

This is a BIG one right? Forgiveness opens your heart and creates more room for prosperity and love to live there. It releases all that is unnecessary and allows goodness to come in. Carrying grudges, resentment, and anger is harmful to us spiritually, mentally, and physically. Let go of old stuff that no longer serves you. Forgiveness = Freedom! That awful ex-husband, let it go. That old boss at that old job, let it go. While you are at it, forgive YOURSELF too. We hold on to all the "shoulda, woulda, couldas," but we must let go in order to move forward. Stop beating yourself up all the time for your mistakes and step into your beautiful life. I know that it is not always easy, but living in the past won't aid in your progress. In order for you to claim your G.I.F.T.S., you have to live in the *present* (pun intended). Let it GO!

TRIUMPHS

> *"Count your blessings. Once you realize how valuable you are and how much you have going for you, the smiles will return, the sun will break out, the music will play, and you will finally be able to move forward in the life that God intended for you with grace, strength, courage, and confidence."*
> -Og Mandino

This is when we get to play a bit! We are so good at paying attention to what we do wrong. *I didn't stick to my diet. I took a wrong turn and got lost. I forgot to pick up something from the store.* I love to ask myself, "What did I do right today?" I guarantee, upon a bit of reflection, you did WAY more right than you did wrong! This is all about giving yourself permission to feel really good. Take some time to sit and reflect on your successes. Where have you come from? What have you overcome?

You must say to yourself, "Well done!" You are fabulous! Where in your life are you triumphant? Think about it: You woke up this morning. HOORAY for you! You got that right. Remember how great you felt when you received a gold star on your schoolwork when you were young? Or how you felt when you thought you deserved one and didn't get it? Well guess what? Get yourself a pack of beautiful shiny gold stars and give them to yourself all the time. I made a delicious dinner, gold star for you. I hugged my kids today, gold star for you. I woke up this morning, gold star for you!

SELF-LOVE

> "Love yourself unconditionally, just as you love
> those closest to you despite their faults"
> -Les Brown

> "Love yourself first and everything else falls
> into line. You really have to love yourself to get
> anything done in this world." -Lucille Ball

YES, Lucy and Les! Self-love is vital to living one's life fully. I truly believe that to give you love is the most important gift of a lifetime. What do you love about yourself? Inside and out? When living in the practice of self-love, you will make very distinct choices. You'll date differently, you'll take care of your health and appearance, and your decisions will come from an inspired place and always in your best interest. YOU should never give up on YOU! How would you live your life if you remembered to always live in love?

Invitation of Self-Love: Ask some good friends and family members to list 5 -10 words or phrases that they would use to describe you. I gave my people the freedom to be real and to be honest! Some of their answers made me laugh, some made me think, but most of all I marveled at how much I was loved. Some of them knew me better than I knew myself! I was reminded that if I was indeed lovable to all these folks, then I could certainly love myself.

In gratitude,

Kim Coles

I Believe in Gratitude

by Precious Bivings

I believe gratitude is the language of those who live in abundance.

I'm grateful that I get to take you on a journey of G.I.F.T.S that begins with Gratitude and ends just the same. My intention is to guide you through what I call unconditional gratitude. During this journey, I'll be sharing parts of my life story as well as the process that was birthed. This same process has been shared on many platforms including the TEDx stage. It was created to help you get unstuck by unbecoming everything you thought you were supposed to be based on what you've experienced so that you can be who you really are. Isn't that an amazing reason to be grateful?

Let's journey…

I was born in 1984 to a beautiful and resilient 15-year-old teenager named Nicole, who was already a mother to a year-old baby boy named Durante. Note: Here is where I get to insert my very first reason to be grateful unconditionally. For a lot of people, this would be a reason to be resentful. However, I'm grateful that I made it here after being hidden in my mother's womb out of shame for almost nine months. I was born to inspire.

By the time I was five years old, I had been taken from my mother, separated from my big brother, and bounced around from house to house. My mother who was only 20 years old was still trying to figure out this thing called life. By the time I turned 10, I had experienced molestation and abandonment, as well verbal and emotional abuse. By 12, I had lost my virginity, become pregnant, and had an abortion all in the same year. *Whew!*

I'm sure you are wondering what in the world does she have to be grateful for? And unconditionally grateful at that? Well here's the deal: Unconditional gratitude is all about having a *no matter what* type of attitude of gratitude. Gratitude requires two things, trust and faith. Even when things are not as you would like them to be, you trust where you've been in your journey and you have faith in where you are going. Trust, by definition, is to have a firm belief in the reliability, truth, ability, or strength of someone or something. Faith, as we know it, is believing in what is to come. Unconditional gratitude requires both. It means more than seeing the cup half full, but being willing to find the silver lining and tying it into a beautiful bow for your gifts to come!

Now back to my journey of unconditional gratitude. Between the ages of 14-16 years old, I became an adult. I was living on my own, sometimes in a house and sometimes homeless. Between 17-27 years old, I'd graduated from Job Corps, become a mother to a beautiful baby girl named Brettani, earned my GED, had been proposed to twice, engaged once, and left with a dress to sell. I'd also opened two businesses, moved across the country, became gainfully employed, promoted several times, and I'd traveled for a reputable company. I had created a life I would be proud of for me and my daughter.

By 31, I had returned to my birth state of South Carolina after an eleven-year hiatus. I founded a non-profit organization; forgave my myself and my past; had the opportunity to have a VIP seat while spending the weekend at the Life You Want Tour starring Oprah, Iyanla, Elizabeth and Deepak; published my first of many books; spoke on the TEDx Greenville stage; opened my own coaching and accountability practice; and kissed many of my dreams in the mouth!

Let's talk about how I arrived at this place of unconditional gratitude, setting beautiful intentions, forgiveness, triumph, and self-love? How was I able to go through the pain, not get stuck in it, and open my gifts? I had to do what I'd like to call *unbecome*. Unbecome is a three-step process: Surrender, work, and live! Let's break down those three steps to unbecoming:

Step 1. Surrender

Surrender and release the expectation of how you thought the situation, the outcome, or how you were supposed to be. Based on what I had experienced in my life, I thought I was supposed to be…nothing. And not just nothing, but whatever lay below nothing. I had to be resilient enough to let go of the idea that I had been domesticated to believe and adapt a new self -perspective—one that included unconditional gratitude!

Surrender is an action word, a word that requires something from you. It guides you to let go and release, to allow it to pass. Whatever it is. Surrender means to cease resistance, saying yes to the journey of life daily. *Why surrender?* Because letting go is how you receive. It's that simple. *To whom would you surrender?* For me it was surrendering to GOD and my soul's mission. For others, including you, it may be surrendering to the universe, the process, and if you're out there on your own, it may be to yourself.

When you think of your own life, what have you experienced that you're still holding on to in a non-serving way? Is it serving you to hold on to it? If your answer is no, let's surrender. In order to have unconditional gratitude, you must be willing to surrender your non-serving perspective of what you've experienced in order to appreciate the lesson.

My greatest opportunity of releasing a non-serving perspective was accepting my mother for who she is versus the mother I wanted her to be. Expecting my mother to be Clair Huxtable, a fictitious perfect TV mom was always unfair to her and disappointing for me. I carried this perspective from my childhood into my adulthood then realized that that perspective/expectation is what was causing so many of our breakdowns and upsets. And when I released that non-serving expectation and accepted my mother for all of who she was (good, bad and unlearned lessons), I was able to experience compassion, love, and a greater hope for an even better relationship. Not only with her, but with everyone who mattered to me. Surrendering what no longer serves was life changing for me.

Step 2 - Work

By definition, work means to actively involve mental or physical effort in order to achieve a purpose or result. The work that I'm referring to is your personal development, which requires that you:

- Set the intentions to create your best self, which ultimately leads to your best life.

- Forgive everyone for everything, especially you.

Being willing to work and journey through your personal development will assist you in becoming the best reflection of yourself by learning the lessons from your life experiences which will assist you gaining a greater appreciation. When you see yourself and life from a manifesting space versus a victim's space, you give yourself the opportunity to grow higher in your gratitude.

Step 3 – Live

What is living and how do I it? Living is subjective. For me, living is being grateful for what I've experienced because it is the very platform I stand on today. It could be a peace of mind and deciding to heal and love again after feeling the pain of being brokenhearted. It's starting a new relationship, retiring from that 9 to 5 to start your own business, learning a new language, traveling across the world, or simply living in unconditional gratitude. Because gratitude is the language of those who live in abundance.

Living in unconditional gratitude is an absolute game changer. In order to live your life from a space of unwavering appreciation no matter what shows up, you'd need to be willing to embrace what's in it for you. When opportunities show up in life that challenge your ability to express unshakable thankfulness, ask yourself: what am I supposed to learn from this, how can I grow from this, what perspective can I see this from that would benefit me? Probing yourself for the opportunity for a higher awareness will allow for you to change your perspective and energy. Allowing yourself to live in complete grate-fulness places you in a position to be open to receive all of the amazingness that awaits you simply because you are grateful unconditionally.

LIFE LESSON:

When you change your perspective, you change your life. Having a mindset of unconditional gratitude is where your abundance lives. Let's go higher!

Joseph's Miracle

by Heidi Deitrich

I believe every woman has the gift of intuition, and a mother's intuition is especially strong and powerful.

GIFT:
GRATITUDE

Learning to listen to your intuition, that inner voice, is often a challenge for those of us who are caretakers, caring about everyone around us, multi-tasking, and wearing a superwoman cape. I have found that one of the greatest gifts we can give ourselves, in order to really open up our intuition, is gratitude. The practice of being grateful becomes habit-forming, automatic, and has the power to be your greatest gift to yourself and those around you, whom you serve. Gratitude has saved me from spiraling down into depression and despair by lifting me up while simultaneously lifting up my 5-year-old son and saving his life.

September 4, 2014. Joseph was starting Kindergarten at a new school. I wasn't even ready for him to go, but little did I know, I was about to have to BE READY for something much bigger—the fight of my life. Just one day later, Joseph was in the ER, diagnosed with a brain tumor the size of a large orange. No sooner did we hear the words "brain tumor" were we admitted into the ICU. It all happened so fast.

Initially, I couldn't bring myself to speak to anyone, other than my husband. I was gathering my strength and my inner resources. I was in a state of shock. Yet, the moment Joseph was rolled into surgery, I had an over-whelming sense of knowing exactly what I needed to do. Without thinking twice, I listened to my inner voice; I followed my intuition.

I had been starting my mornings with writing in my gratitude journal for some time. The energy had spilled over into my daily living, seeing gratitude in the simplest things throughout my day. Incredibly, the whole summer leading up to Joseph's diagnosis, I was being drawn to read books about cancer, NDEs (near death experiences), and miraculous healings, and I didn't know why. There was an unexplainable, gravitational pull for me to read these books. I took pictures of them all on my iPhone: Dr. Wayne Dyer's *Wishes Fulfilled*, Anita Moorjani's *Dying to Be Me*, Eben Alexander's *Proof of Heaven*, and Todd Burpo's *Heaven Is for Real*. The photo of *Wishes Fulfilled* was dated August 6, 2014—one month and one day before Joseph was admitted to the ICU. I had underlined, made margin notes, and highlighted Wayne's words of feeling "pulled" and "tugged" to read certain books and write certain words, which he called "channeled writing."

It was the message that I got from *Heaven Is for Real* that was the most impactful and what stuck in my head, as Joseph was being wheeled into surgery. The message was, in times of our greatest need (to heal our children), reach out to our community for prayer because there's tremendous power in prayer in numbers. I had a strong inner urgency to read the book on our eight-hour drive home from a family beach vacation. Unable to put it down, I underlined and took endless notes. I was pulled to read it right then, feeling like I needed to study it. I still remember the anxiety I felt in that moment. It was really crazy!

As I read, I said out loud, "Oh, no. We're so screwed. If anything ever happens to one of our children, like this boy, we have no church community to reach out to for prayers." Weeks later, when Joseph went into the ICU, I prayed like I never prayed before. The message from the book rang strong in my head. I said nothing publicly until Joseph went in for his surgery. In that moment, I knew exactly what I needed to do. I knew it was time to break my silence. I was being called to reach out to as many people that I could, and I knew Facebook would be my greatest source of community since we didn't have that big church family.

I encourage you to listen to your own inner voice, your intuition. Pay attention to your thoughts and your inner pulls. *Heaven is for Real* taught me that the power of prayer is absolutely amazing, that the power of faith and belief is miraculous, and that miracles happen every day. The following italicized print are my actual Facebook posts:

<u>September 8, 2014</u>

Thank you all for the tremendous outpouring of love, thoughts, prayers and words to lift us up. Fran and I are so incredibly grateful and appreciative. I am so grateful I can be here with Joseph 24/7, sleeping alongside him in his bed. All things considered, Joseph is doing amazing. He is quite the trooper. Please keep Joseph in your prayers. Pray that big tumor was benign; Pray that there is absolutely no sign of any of it remaining; Pray that he will be fully functioning, back to a normal life of a happy, healthy 5-year old real soon. Thank you all from the bottom of our hearts. We appreciate every prayer and every word. They all mean so much, as they lift Joseph up and give us strength.

I recognize now that it was gratitude that was getting me through, combined with unwavering faith and choosing hope. I only ever saw an outcome of health and healing for Joseph. I was grateful for the prayers and outpouring of love and connection and for every little thing around us. This was all I allowed to enter my mind. Never once was there a thought of, "Why him? Why me?" I'm not sure I would have automatically followed that thought process years ago, before consciously practicing gratitude.

<u>September 9, 2014</u>

As I lie here in Joseph's room in ICU, my sweet baby is finally asleep, after a long post-op night last night and a long day today... I finally have an opportunity to sleep, but I can't. I watch his every breath. I listen for any moan of discomfort or for his sweet little voice calling out, "Mom." Yet, I feel so blessed.

From outside our window I can hear the seemingly constant near-deafening noise of the medevac helicopter landing, with a clear view of them coming and going. Every day, I count the landings. Each time we are in disbelief at the number of children coming here in a life-threatening, near death status, and I am grateful. I have my child here with me. Fran and I walked into the ER with a seemingly very healthy-looking little boy. In fact, the doctors were shocked at how well he looked once they found the tumor in his head. Yes, they elevated him to ICU and scheduled him for emergency surgery, but they had some time to do the tests. Time to pull together their "A Team," as they called it. They felt it was critical enough to operate on Sunday, rather than wait until Monday, but they had time to make the plan. I feel blessed that Joseph is at this amazing hospital, with such amazing doctors and nurses and staff. I feel blessed that I can be here with him 24/7. I feel blessed that each step has gone as we had hoped and prayed for.

I believe in the power of prayer. I believe that there is

strength in numbers. Please, please, please keep praying for sweet Joseph... we're not out of the woods yet. Thank you all so much.

Many people followed Joseph's story through to the miraculous point of hearing, "No further treatment is needed," and connected with me, asking, "Why do you think this happened? What are you supposed to teach from this?" Though I'm still not exactly sure, I do know that I'm meant to help other families and I feel a strong urgency to share this lesson that I learned:

LIFE LESSON:

Gratitude has the power to transform. When you're in the habit of the practice, when you need it the most, it will already be automatic thought process, even in your darkest hours. With gratitude, we are brought to a more peaceful, calmer place. This allows you to listen to your inner voice; for that inner voice is not just a passing thought. That thought is actually God speaking to you, giving you instructions to follow. Trust it. Listen to it. Follow it. A mother's intuition is especially strong, so it's important to give yourself the time and the space, even if it's just five minutes a day, to slow down and sit quietly, thinking and writing about what you're grateful for. Our intuition is divinely rooted in our gratitude, where we find that sense of groundedness and where answers and direction come to us.

Can We Win a Bipolar Depression Fight?

by Kathleen Lynch

I believe my battle scars are my badges in my fight against bipolar depression.

GIFT:
TRIUMPHS

I want share with you what I believe has helped me function pretty well in society with a bipolar depression diagnosis. It took years of struggle to get as stable as I have been for about 20 years now. I am 54 years old and my first hospitalization was in 1982 when I was 20 years old. I come from a large, middle-class black family and grew up with many things I feel blessed for. I am the youngest of seven children, spanning over 21 years.

One of the first major tragedies I experienced was the loss of my father, a Chicago policeman, when I was only 7. The impact of that loss was subtle at the time, but it has shaped the course of my life, and one of my older brother's life, with weighted impact. Losing my father took its toll on us because my mother never dealt with it or showed any emotion. We never worked through the grief process. No one even showed any emotion. I feel like in some way we lost both our father and our mother when my daddy died.

My brother Tim actively attempted to fill the void by becoming the man of the house, a very tall order for an eleven year old. He was quite good at it for a while, but eventually he self-medicated with street drugs and a gambling addiction. I filled my mother's need for companionship. I was her shadow during my childhood and teen years. Instead of coming into my own and exploring my identity, I tried to be the good girl. My facade of maturity was really just a mask, and in my adulthood her firm grip on me was hard to break free from.

My mother was such a caring mom, and she believed we should all have the best education. We were raised Catholic, and all of my older siblings went to Catholic schools. I, however, got very sick in the first grade and was hospitalized with pneumonia. My mom kept me home the rest of that school year, so when I re-entered first grade, at the nearby public school, I was a year behind. Thankfully, that too was a very good public school.

I mention this background to let you know one of the things that I believe colored my past and my first manic episode. I excelled in school and was able to skip sixth grade, so I was no longer behind a year. Always in the back of my mind, though, was a sense of not being able to keep up with the rest of my family, all of whom excelled academically and athletically.

My first episode happened after I was working for the second summer as an Inroads Summer Intern at Harris Bank. The first summer went pretty well, but I did get very weepy and depressed that first year, because, again, I felt like I didn't measure up. I also had waited what seemed like a lifetime to prove myself and to live like an adult. What I found was the little child inside stays there and never leaves. When I was young, I seemed very mature to my peers, but as I have grown older, I sometimes feel more like that child I never allowed myself to be. Glowing reviews from my mentor and those I worked with were not enough to satisfy me in my striving for perfection. I went back to my second year of college at Loyola University in Chicago with hope and eagerness.

That second summer came, and I was ready to get back to it. What happened was strange to me. I came in on that first day, ready to work. For some reason, the words "you are just like your brother" set me off. You see, my older siblings all paved the way for me. Everywhere I went, someone knew one of my siblings at the bank. Many knew my brothers, Tim and Tony—both apples in my mother's eye, her golden boys. They excelled academically and in sports, and were just all around nice guys.

When the second summer of what was supposed to be my four-year internship came, I was ready to get back to work at the bank. At the bank, my summer internship assignment was to develop a training manual for new hires. I was asked to put together a training manual for others and work with Nate, who went to high school with my brother Tim. Nate made the comment, and all of a sudden I was on top of the world. But I spiraled completely up and out the door. Unfortunately, I can't explain how or why it happened. It just did. I went from feeling unstoppable to completely incapable. That is when the racing thoughts started and when going without sleep began. Before I knew it, I was delusional think things started and stop by me and for me. It did get scary.

My mother got me to the hospital and I was afraid of being locked up forever, so I tried to escape. They restrained me and the vicious cycle began. Interestingly, others who were hospitalized with me were amazed by my quick transformation. I entered the facility in one state of mind and after only a couple days, I was fine. My hospital stays, including that one, only lasted about two weeks, but I had one every year for the next six years.

I still finished college in four years, and I kept working my first job, Marshal Fields department store, for a few years after graduating. Later, I got a job working in the marketing department of Soft Sheen Products, but I blew that one and all of the wonderful shots I got after that. My lack of compliance at those times cost me many of my career aspirations. When a manic episode hit, I would lose touch with reality. It cost me career-oriented jobs because with lack of sleep and becoming delusional I couldn't perform the duties of the job. I needed to be hospitalized. When you feel good, you begin to believe you don't need any medication and stop taking it. Often, quite innocently, too, I'd just plain forget to take it at times. This all led to my yearly relapses, which is typical for most with bipolar.

This isn't to say I didn't hold jobs, however, because I did. I am most grateful for my resiliency and my ability to bounce back. I continued to work through temporary agencies or at jobs I could have done right out of high school. There was hardly a time when I wasn't working at least one job, but most of the time a job and a half. To this day, I still work two jobs while pursuing my dream of becoming an author and wellness coach.

After several years of struggle, I finally stabilized. I stopped fighting the bipolar disorder and called a truce. While I acknowledge and accept that I may forever be affected in some way by this condition, I now do all I can to remain focused on my health and stay compliant with my medication. I see a therapist every other week and my psychiatrist every three months. What helps most though is getting enough rest, eating healthy, and exercising. I wake up every day and think of five things I am grateful for. I journal my thoughts and talk with a friend when I get down. Doing things for others takes my mind off of me too. Consequently, I have had very little trouble in terms of side effects except for weight gain.

My goal now is to help erase the stigma of being bipolar. We are in great company. Many gifted people, including celebrities and innovators, have had this diagnosis or showed signs of it. I have found a spiritual connection that seems to heighten when symptomatic. It can feel like an alternate world. When managed well, it feels like a close connection to my Heavenly Father. When out of control, it can be terrifying. You don't know or understand your own strength. Or whose side you're on. But when managed well, I feel a very close, loving connection to my Heavenly Father and a source of strength I can share with others. Instead of trying to beat bipolar depression, learn how to live with it and benefit from the special gift it offers.

LIFE LESSON:

Though I may never win my fight, I can strike up a truce and have some amnesty granted.

Speak from the Heart

by Lee Tkachuk

I believe that everyone needs to speak well. You have an excellent message, but no one will hear it if you don't deliver it.

My nickname as a kid was "Motormouth," and it fit me well. I could to talk to anyone, any time, in any situation, and I talked a LOT. My parents used to tease that I didn't even stop talking while sleeping. I also had the unique talent, or so I thought, of being able to talk my way into or out of any situation, something that I thought was cool, but my siblings and cousins did not.

As I got older, I stayed true to my nickname. Born without the fear-of-speaking gene, I was often the first to raise my hand in class. Yep, I was that annoying person who volunteered to go first for any oral presentation. I didn't get nervous, didn't sweat, didn't panic. It had gone from simply being a part of me to something I loved to do.

Some of my friends would get so worked up they would become physically sick. I think some of them would have rather walked across a bed of nails than give a presentation, but I was comfortable with them. I followed the same process every time I had to present, from grade school through middle school and all through high school and college.

I would start with a topic, write an outline, and then fill in details. I'd practice to get my timing down and would adjust it to be longer or shorter, depending on the requirements for the speech. I would practice it everywhere, every chance I had, until the big day. I knew those presentations inside out and had every word, every pause, and every point memorized. I practiced so much that I never needed notes or cheat sheets. I always got an A, and my friends constantly asked me for help. I could help with the process, but it was up to them to practice. No matter what I told them though, or how I helped them, I couldn't erase the panic they felt when going to the front of the class.

I thought that speaking was easy and because I was not nervous or panicked, I assumed I would also be successful, as long as I was prepared. After all, if you have something memorized and you practice hard, success is guaranteed. Right?

My college years were pretty typical for the mid-1980s.

My school was three hours from home, and I came home a few times each semester, got decent (okay, not really decent, but passing) grades, and had a lot of fun. I was in a sorority, had a lot of friends, and a very active social life. Everything was golden.

My teachers liked me, I had a lot of friends, and I became a pro at cooking mac n' cheese and ordering pizza. I took a few speech classes and volunteered to give presentations whenever asked. I still used the same process, and I think at one point my roommates were REALLY sick of hearing me practice all the time. I didn't know where speaking was going to fit into my life; I just knew it was something I was good at without trying.

A few years after college, I was asked to give the introduction for an award being given to a friend of mine, Liz. I wasn't nervous about presenting, but this was big. There were over 500 people expected, and this was a huge deal for her. We were college roommates who grew to become good friends, and I looked up to her. She was an amazing person—one of those people who was always happy, and it wasn't an act. She could see the silver lining in any situation and could spot the smallest patch of blue sky on a cloudy day. Beautiful inside and out, things came easily to her.

It hadn't always been that way, though. Her childhood was rough. Her father was abusive, and he left Liz and her six brothers and sisters to be raised by their mother when Liz was only five years old.

In 1969, a lot of women were stay-at-home moms and wives, and that's all her mother had ever known. She had not gone to college, had never worked, and depended on her husband for everything. She had never made major decisions or financial decisions, paid a bill, or disciplined her kids. All she had to do was keep the house clean, have a hot meal on the table every night, and be a perfect wife.

As a result of the abuse her husband doled out—both physical and emotional—she was a wreck when he left, and she had a nervous breakdown. The kids were split up. Liz went to live with her grandparents, one of her brothers went to live with an aunt and uncle, and the older ones were sent to an orphanage. They weren't technically orphans, as both parents were living, but their father was not around and their mother was incapable of living alone or raising children. It wasn't easy on any of them.

Liz was the lucky one. Her grandparents were amazing and made sure that she was well taken care of, that school was a priority, and that she was loved. When they passed away during her late teens, Liz took everything they taught her and made something of her life. She volunteered, worked with kids, and was a genuinely nice person, someone her grandparents would have been proud of.

Now she was getting an award, and it was up to me to introduce her—to list her accomplishments and tell the audience what a wonderful person she was. It was up to me to give them details and to map out the reasons why she was so deserving of their award. It was up to me to show them what a truly special, amazing, hard-working, caring, compassionate person she was.

I worked on the introduction for weeks, in secret when she wasn't around. Practicing it on lunch breaks and in my car. Then I went home and practiced some more. I had a good speech written, every word of it memorized, and I knew the audience was going to love Liz as much as I did. Then the big night arrived. By this time, Liz knew she was getting the award and that I was introducing her, but she had no idea what I was going to say. I was, for the first time, a little nervous. This was SO important to me.

I walked to the front of the room, stood behind the podium ...

And froze.

I couldn't move. I couldn't say a word. I couldn't remember anything I had memorized. I just stood there.

Time stood still. The room was quiet. Every eye was on me, and I couldn't remember even one word that I had memorized. I didn't have any notes with me. Why should I? I knew every syllable by heart until that moment. In that moment, I couldn't even remember my own name.

The silence in the room seemed to go forever, and, still, no one was moving. You could hear a pin drop. I had no idea what to do. This had never happened to me.

I was Motormouth who could talk to anyone at any time about anything. Why couldn't I talk now or even form words? I was paralyzed.

Just then, I heard a whisper just to the left of me. A woman I had never met came up to the podium under the pretense of fixing my microphone and whispered four magic words: "Speak from the heart."

And that's exactly what I did. I started with the story of Liz's childhood and everything she had done to help others. I spoke about how amazing and giving she was, and the many ways she inspired others. I let the audience fall in love with her and helped them welcome her to the stage with standing applause. I had done what I had set out to do, but without my practiced speech, notes, or anything I had memorized. I spoke from the heart.

We lost Liz in 2009 after a battle with cancer. She had done so much during her short 45 years, more than most people who live to 100. She touched the lives of many, but that night, 20 years earlier, she gave me the gift of my future, my career, my passion. Being able to speak about someone so precious to me, someone I was close to, until her last breath, was the start of my passion for speaking. Liz gave me the gift of speaking from the heart.

Speaking in front of an audience, either personally or professionally, should not be over-rehearsed or mechanical. Instead, it should be a process that includes real-life stories and humor, prepared, organized and practiced, but NEVER memorized. Speak from the heart, and you will be successful in everything you do. We all have a story. What's yours?

LIFE LESSON:

Speak from the heart. Your light will shine bright, the words will ring true, and your audience will love you.

5 Easy Steps to Change Your Life

by Ashley Ann

I believe in my unlimited prosperity and success.

I hope you soon will believe in yours too. We each have many gifts and talents. The gifts I received in my late twenties are the reasons for my current success. The astounding thing about these gifts is that they are given to everyone on the planet. So I shouldn't say I received my gifts in my late twenties, but instead they were activated. You can activate yours right now. Accountability, creativeness, and manifestation funnel into **Intention**. Intention has allowed me to do what I love: travel, making new connections, having fun, and helping to build businesses. I am a part of others' success every day.

I believe you were energetically drawn to this book and to this chapter because you are ready to activate your Gift of Intention and really live. Every day I wake up and thank God for my current life. This is a big change. I used to wake up depressed with puffy eyes and a racing, restless mind, wondering if God even loved me anymore. If God loved me, I wondered, why am I going through all of this? Had I been really horrible and was experiencing karma? I wanted to die from all of the pain I was in. I confess: I was suicidal. I know a good Christian girl is not supposed to have those thoughts, but I did, and I know I'm not the only person who has been there.

I was married to a man who cheated on me constantly. Sometimes he didn't come home for days. I couldn't escape the thought of marriage, because I own a wedding and event design company. It's all about love and marriage! I can laugh about it now, by the way, but I couldn't then. My health was horrible. I was about 85 pounds overweight, my doctor was telling me my spine was deteriorating, and I needed to prepare for a wheelchair. The woman who I thought was my best friend at one time in life had formed a relationship with my then husband, and he drained our account and took his mistress on a Christmas trip. On top of that, I lost three huge contracts in one month. Needless to say, I was not in a good place.

I was so ashamed of my life and of what was happening in my marriage. I didn't tell anyone what I was going through though. I made a decision to go out and lie every day. The reason I say I lied is because I was pretending to be okay and that things were good at home. I was pretending that business was fine while trying to keep up regular spending habits because I did not want people to know I was sinking. You're probably wondering how I ended up in that predicament.

That is exactly what I thought one day after my ex-husband and I got into a physical altercation (as in two adults physically fighting and throwing things at one another). As I lay on the floor crying and asking God to just kill me, I heard the words of my grandpa. He always said, "Do you want to be right or do you want to be happy?" It was as clear as a bell. I was spending so much time trying to be right and wanting to make everyone believe I was doing well. In reality, I was miserable. I was so concerned with what other people thought of me, living a lie every day. I walked out the house looking beautiful, smiling, and even had the audacity to comfort other people (lol) when I was the one who needed comforting and a reality check.

It is true that my ex-husband, and ex best friend mistreated me. It is true that I had a bad business deal with an un-honorable person, but do you know what else was true? I allowed these things! This is the part no one likes to admit. I had to figure out how I had gotten to such a miserable life. The truth is no matter how terrible other people were to me, it didn't matter. It didn't matter because we can't control other people. We can't control what they think, how they act, what they do or don't do. If you take accountability, you will realize what I realized. I was the one who allowed it.

Why do we stay in terrible relationships? Why do we let people take advantage of us? Why do we let ourselves become overweight? Why are we afraid to take a new path or meet new people? There is no reason to. We literally have everything inside of us to become successful and create the life we want to live. Success is nothing more than an accomplishment of aim or purpose, in laymen terms. Success is a person who gets what they want. This is where manifestation comes into play, and it's a lot easier than you think. Here's how to change your life in five simple steps and intentionally gain prosperity and success:

1. **Write down what is crappy about your life**. Take out a piece of paper and write down what is not hot about your life. If we want to change things we have to assess them. The first step to a solution is admitting there is a problem. Don't dwell on this because you are going to change them sooner than you think.

2. **Write down what is awesome, good, and okay about your life.** This is important because you don't want to slip into condemnation. Everyone does something right. Each of us has good in us, and we are all important to someone. No matter how bad you think your life is, even if all you can say is that you are alive. That is enough. Everyday living is another opportunity.

3. **Tell yourself the truth about everything you have done to contribute to your current situation.** This is where accountability comes into play. It is very easy to point the finger and focus on how someone hurt you, disrespected you, or disappointed you. In some cases, it may not be a person. You may be suffering from poor health, but I guarantee you can change the experience based on your actions. You want to be accountable, so you don't repeat unfavorable actions. You must use favorable actions so you can have favorable outcomes.

4. **Write down the life you want**. Sometimes you are down so long you forget your dreams. They seem so far away. When you write down the vision for your life, it puts you one step closer to obtaining it. You are physically participating in changing your life when you write down your ideal life. Put down everything, no matter how trivial you think it may be. This is the beginning of manifestation.

5. **Create your action plan**. This is all about being intentional and creative. Pick three to seven of the things you said you want for your new life. Now write down another three to seven simple things that will get you to your overall goal. For example: I wanted to be financially stable, so my action plan included: becoming a better networker

by meeting three new people per week, joining a new business organization, starting to post on Facebook 3x a week, only eating out once a week, and finding a way to cut overhead costs in my office space.

There is nothing difficult about anything in the action plan. I intentionally did each one of those steps every week. I was intentional and determined to be consistent. I started to get creative with where I would meet new people and what I considered a networking event. Within 60 days, I closed eight new contracts. I simply decided to live intentionally. I picked small goals that were easy to accomplish and within six months, I completely changed my life. I got out of a bad marriage, lost weight, moved to a new place, and improved my health (which I'm proud to say I'm not close to being in a wheelchair now).

I started looking for new office space, which led to me opening my second location, and most importantly I was happy and free. I wasn't bound by any shame or pain anymore. I was actually living the life I wanted and you should too. I know if I can change my life, you can change yours. We all have the power to live with Intention. You have everything inside of you to live the life you want to live.

LIFE LESSON:

Whether we want to admit it or not, we always have a part to play in life's outcomes. Misery and motivation are a choice. Take assessment of how you contributed to each situation you are in. This will ensure you life happier and fuller. We have the power to create whatever life we want. Everything you need is already inside of you; you just have to turn it on and use it. Trying times and hurdles are nothing more than motivation and an opportunity for you to show your tenacity, strength, and brilliance.

AGAINST ALL ODDS: A Survivor's Story of Hope

by Melanie Anderson

I believe God has a purpose for my life.

My transformational journey began in 2009, shortly after my divorce. I remember like it was yesterday. By the time my divorce was final, on one hand, there was a sigh of relief, but on the other hand, I was a single parent of three young kids, a college student, full-time employee, and depressed.

I felt like a failure and was not pleased with the examples I was setting for my children. It had been my goal to make sure my children had a father figure in the home, and I felt like I let them down. Not only did I let my children down, but I was disgusted with myself and the bad decisions I had made up to that point. So I made it a priority to work on having more of a personal relationship with God. I did some soul searching and prayed continuously for answers, and my ultimate prayer was not only for God to reveal to me what I was doing wrong and why I was making these mistakes, but to show me how to be a better person, mother, daughter, and friend. I decided to surrender my will for God's will. Now, let me tell you that this transformation did not happen overnight. It was a long process.

My first assignment was to do a serious self-evaluation. This was by far one of the hardest things I had to do. I mean, to look at myself in the mirror and see a person who is supposed to be responsible for being an example to my children and wanting them to have a much better life than I did was not working out too well. Things were actually getting worse and falling apart. To see someone in the mirror who was a disappointment and made tons of mistakes as a mother such as: not choosing the right men, being reactive instead of proactive when it came to helping my troubled teen, unknowingly putting things or people before my kids at times, and not being wise enough to understand what was really best for myself let alone my children was heartbreaking. I began asking God for wisdom and to show me how to be a better mother. I also had to let go of everything I was holding onto: past hurts, unforgiveness, shame, and disappointments. I did not know who I was anymore.

I had been a people pleaser for years, so I asked God to deliver me from people, their opinions, and perception of me. People were judging me and my situation instead of teaching me the right thing, offering suggestions on how to get back on track or extending grace. They had no idea of the internal struggle that was going on, the massive guilt I endured, or perhaps that I was just simply doing the best I knew how to do at that time.

One of the biggest things I discovered was that I lost myself. I was in my own way. I experienced a lot of eye-opening experiences during this process. I wish I could tell you this process was easy, but it was hard and there were no shortcuts. It was now time for me to learn how to be single, happy, and content, or like my granny would say when she was alive, "Get somewhere and sit down!"

I had been working a corporate job that I loved for several years. I was very passionate about the service I provided, but I still felt unfulfilled. I decided to switch from being a part-time college student to a full-time student, which was harder than I thought. While in college, I definitely faced my fair share of several unexpected challenges. In June 2011, I received some devastating news. I had been sick for quite some time and didn't really tell anyone. After my third biopsy, I returned to my dermatologist shortly after vacation for my results. The doctor walked in the room, and I was playing a game on my phone thinking the appointment would be no big deal. I'd get a prescription and call it a day, I thought. Needless to say, I was wrong!

"Your biopsy and blood work has tested positive for

two forms of Lupus," she said. "Lupus?! You mean the kind of Lupus people die from?" I asked. She said yes and I lost it. How am I going to tell my kids I have Lupus? I told her my aunt passed away from complications related to Lupus and cried my eyes out. I was so nervous my hands were shaking as she gave me a copy of my test results. She tried reminding me that it wasn't a death sentence, but I was no longer listening to her. I was in total shock! I cannot recall the drive home, but I knew I had a paper due for school, so I didn't have the time or the energy to focus on Lupus. It was a hard pill to swallow, and it took a while for me to accept it.

To make matters worse, I was on a three-month waiting list to see a rheumatologist. I kept telling myself, "You have got to tell your mother," but every time I rehearsed what I would say and how to say it, the word "Lupus" would tear me up. My plan was to wait until my doctor's appointment, so I could become strong enough to say it without sounding sad and leading others to worry. Plus, I'd have more information about the disease. Time passed and this became my secret for over a month.

The diagnosis really took me to a dark place. There were times I couldn't find the words to pray, so some days I just laid in bed. Other days I got on my knees, but no words came out, just tears. When I'd get emotional at work, I would clock out and drive to Walgreens parking lot on my lunch break, sit in my car for an hour listening to gospel music, and just cry.

That reminded me that there is always a secret place that I can go to and cry out to God. I got in my closet, stretched out over the floor, and just wept and pleaded with God to heal me. When I stopped crying, I continued to lay there in complete silence. A still, small voice said, "Everything is not happening to you, it's happening for your good and my grace is sufficient." Initially, I thought this was my death sentence. I decided that if I was going to die from this, then I needed to start living. I began wondering what my life would mean after it ended. From there, I started thinking that there had to be more to life than working a 9 to 5. I wanted the dash between the year I was born and the year I died to mean something.

One day, I was listening to Steve Harvey on the radio and he asked, "What would you do if you knew you couldn't fail?" Once I accepted the diagnosis, a fire lit within me. I realized life is too short. *It's time to follow my dreams of becoming an actress*! I changed my way of thinking and realized Lupus saved me! Lupus gave me a reason to live and fight. Lupus gave me permission to be fearless and finally follow my dreams. Despite all my challenges, I graduated from LeMoyne-Owen College with a Bachelor's degree in Business Administration on May 12, 2012.

I also decided to focus on my acting career. I drove from Memphis to Atlanta every other weekend for acting classes. Determined more than ever, I decided to step out on faith and leave my corporate job of 10 years. I relocated to Atlanta and experienced several obstacles, but didn't get side-tracked. I kept telling myself if you can deal with the 24-hour affects of Lupus, then nothing else can stop you. Eventually, I booked my first commercial and went on to book my first role in a TV series for BET in 2013, earning my first acting credit. My most recent appearance is a guest-starring role in TV One's hit television show, *Fatal Attraction*.

I created a vision board of everything God spoke to me to stay on track. Now I am an actress, inspirational speaker, co-author, and entrepreneur. God has given me a vision and blessed me to start my own business. When I look back over my life, I realize all the mistakes I made shaped me into the woman I am today. I am overjoyed and grateful, and I love sharing my experiences to inspire, uplift, and encourage other women and teenagers to never give up on their dreams despite their circumstances.

LIFE LESSON:

There is no time limit on pursuing your dreams.

Live Life with Good Intentions

by Shade Adu

I believe that we must be intentional with words we speak into our lives and the lives of others.

Our thoughts are forces that have the ability to transform and destroy. They can transform into words that can influence the decisions we make in life, so we must be aware of this power and operate with intention in our daily lives.

Think of a friend or a family member you have (or had) who was labeled the "bad child." They heard this from their parents, siblings, other family members, their teachers, and peers. Soon, the child begins emulating the "bad child" characteristics, which all started out as a thought that manifested into a grim reality.

Like the story of the bad child, you have the power to create the life of your dreams or become the constructor of a personal nightmare. Every day that we have breath in our body is another opportunity to be grateful and act with the best intentions in mind. Your thoughts can spark change. Your actions can save lives. Don't take this gifting lightly, because your gifts can be taken away.

I remember growing up as a loquacious little girl in Irvington, New Jersey. I loved to talk and I loved to laugh. I could go on and on for hours and be extremely content while getting lost in my own thoughts. My mother saw this as a gift and encouraged me to speak. She also looked for opportunities within her fixed budget to keep my mind stimulated. These early seeds of confidence, affirmation, and encouragement have been cultivated and have powerfully blossomed throughout the years.

My mother constantly reminded me of the power of my voice and being intentional with my gifts. These lessons have stayed with me throughout my life. I remember a time when my gifts felt more like an inconvenience. From a very young age, I'd always been a voice of reason. One day my friends and I were playing and I lectured them about how they should behave and be in life. They thought I was bossy. In retrospect, I realize that I was wise beyond my years, but my peers did not understand me. I was a unicorn. So they told me to shut up. They walked away and refused to listen to me. My feelings were crushed, and I vowed to never speak or use my voice of reason again.

"Who am I to think that I can provide value to the world? *Who are you not to?"*

Two days after my vow of silence, I conveniently lost my voice. All that came out were unpleasant shrieks and uneventful attempts to project my voice, resulting in painful whispers. My noiselessness was so bad that people really didn't want me to speak, so I carried a notepad and pen to communicate my thoughts at school.

Later that day, I was called to the principal's office, who announced that I had won a special award. As a bonus of winning this award, I would have the honor of giving a speech at graduation. I was selected out of 800 students to give this award in front of my friends, family, teachers, and over 5000 other people present. This was a major honor for an eighth grader.

I was ecstatic! But when I opened my mouth to accept my principal's offer, nothing came out. My voice was gone. The gift that my mother told me to keep was gone. I then remembered how just a couple of days prior, I had vowed to not use it again. And voilà...just like that it was gone. I hoped, prayed and diligently worked to get my voice back in time for graduation. I seriously believe that God has a sense of humor because I lost what I neglected and, within two days, begged for it back. Luckily, after a couple of days, it came back and I gave the most epic middle school graduation speech ever.

I share this story because I know what it feels like to just exist in life with no intent. We say things to ourselves as if words have no meaning or power. Our words must be used for good because our words speak life. Our gifts are not meant to be hoarded for ourselves. They are supposed to be shared. You are a blessing to someone who is impatiently waiting for your light.

This story has stayed with me for over a decade and I am constantly reminded that my voice matters. Our words have consequences and we can't afford to take that lightly. Wear your crown proudly and allow your light to shine. Your one voice could make the world of difference to someone else.

My gift has since taken me around the world. I used my voice to pay for college and graduate school. I used it to travel to speak, and teach and train educators. I share my gift daily on Periscope and across social media platforms. When I was just that little girl in the small 2.5-mile Township of Irvington, NJ, I couldn't see where my gifts were going to take me. I had no idea where God was going to send me. Today, I am more intentional and spend time cultivating my gifts and surrounding myself with other leaders who affirm my voice.

During this journey of life, it is imperative to find good people who are willing to journey with you. You can't and shouldn't do this alone. I am grateful for all of the people who have helped me because I would not be where I am without them. Cherish the people around you and capture as many positive memories as possible. Our time is limited on this Earth, so I try my best to enjoy every second of every day.

Speaking your gifts is about speaking your truth. You must be open and honest with yourself in order to evolve. Your gifts are just that—your gifts. They are not necessarily for everyone else. There will be people who will ignore you. However, there are millions who need you and are waiting for you to rise into the person you were destined to be. They need you to be strong, gracious, and intentional.

Being more intentional requires information and implementation. Attend events, read books, and connect with people that empower you. However, information isn't enough. You must implement and take bold and consistent action. If you want to write that book, pick up a pen and paper and start writing. If you want to go back to school, start researching your options. If you want to start a business, find a mentor who can help. Your dream won't work unless you do. God honors action takers. Information is the foundation of your intent while implementation is the manifestation of that intent. Intent in action is powerful. It is a way of sharing your gifts with those who need it the most.

Remember, your gifts have never really been about you. They are supposed to be given, shared, and passed on to the next generation of speakers, leaders, and bossy girls on the playground. They need to see you exist, so that they can give themselves permission to exist. Your gifts matter and you are destined for significance. So stand up tall. Put those big girl panties on and speak your

GIFTS. The world is waiting for your unique contribution and they can't wait any longer.

LIFE LESSON:

"Your beliefs become your thoughts,
Your thoughts become your words,
Your words become your actions,
Your actions become your habits,
Your habits become your values,
Your values become your destiny."

— Mahatma Gandhi

Purposed Intended

by LaKesha L. Williams

I believe everything that happens to me has an intended purpose. I just have to discover that purpose, which is my gift to others.

Intention: a thing intended; an aim or plan

Purpose: the reason for which something is done or created

When I was around five years old, I was raped by a boy who lived in my neighborhood who was about three years older than me. I clearly remember the events of that day. It was warm enough outside for kids to be out playing in the apartment complex that I lived in with my mom, dad and older brother. As I'd often do, I went outside with my brother and played with his friends' younger siblings. I don't recall if it was a school day or if it was summer time, but I do remember all the neighborhod kids getting together and playing a game of hide-and-go-seek.

When there were too many kids, we'd hide in pairs so the game wouldn't be so hard and wouldn't go on forever. There was no particular method that we had of choosing partners other than whoever was closest to you. I just happened to be closest to a boy who was my older brother's friend. He grabbed my arm and took off running into the woods behind the apartments along with the other children and their partners.

His hand was damp and sticky with sweat. He ran with my arm in hand the whole time, basically pulling me along. It seemed like we ran for a while because my legs were tired, my arm hurt, and the screams of the other children were beginning to become distant. Finally, we stopped running and I rested against a nearby tree. I was tired, but still caught up in the excitement of the game. The thrill of wondering if we'd be found or never be found and winning was all I could think about. I trusted that since we had run so far we would win, but little did I know my partner had more sinister plans.

After I caught my breath, I still wondered where exactly we were supposed to be hiding because it seemed we were just standing behind trees, which wasn't a good hiding spot. While I was busy looking back, I don't remember what he was doing, but when I turned and stood up to see where he was, he was right in my face. He put both hands on the tree and pressed himself into me, further pushing me against the tree. He was so close that his lips were almost touching mine, and I could feel his hot breath on my face. He was breathing hard and slow, and I felt like I was going to suffocate from him pressing me into the tree and from the funk of his breath, smelling like old hotdogs and underarm pits.

As I turned away to try and get some fresh air, he grabbed my face and tried to kiss me. I held my lips together tightly in disgust. I felt his tongue trying to force its way into my mouth followed by teeth and spit. I cannot recall what happened between the kiss and what came next or how or when we moved from against the tree, but what I do remember next is that we were standing by a ravine that I hadn't noticed before. There was a slight drop with what I remember as a stream of water at the bottom. He stood behind me holding both my arms and saying in a low husky voice, "If you scream, I will throw you down there and alligators will eat you." His lips touched my right ear as he talked. I was terrified and all I could think about was the alligators eating me.

I was paralyzed with fear. This boy was taller and bigger than me. Something inside of me said run, but my legs would not work. Again, all I could think about was the alligators and I still had no clue what was about to come next. He laid a jacket he had on the ground. To this day I don't remember him having a jacket on or where he got the jacket from, only that it was red. He told me to lay down on my stomach.

The ground was cool and hard. I heard leaves

crunching, so maybe it was fall outside. I also remember the smell of dirt as I laid there wondering what was coming next. He straddled me from behind and began grinding himself against me. I still didn't really know what was going on. I felt like I couldn't breathe from his weight on me and at this point the side of my face was in the cool dirt. He kissed my neck a few times before stopping. Then, I had no idea what he was doing. Looking back, I now know that he was unbuttoning his pants, because he pulled my pants and underwear down next.

I was still lying flat on my stomach as he repositioned himself so that our skin touched. He began grinding his little man parts against my little bottom. Once he became fully erect and figured out what he was doing, he penetrated me and I blacked out. I don't know when he stopped, but my memory picks back up as we are walking through the woods back home. It was getting dark outside.

He walked me back to the edge of the woods where he reminded me that he'd throw me in the ravine with the alligators if I told anyone. Afterwards, he ran off and left me standing there, so I slowly walked back to my building where I was met by my mother who was furious because she had been looking for me. It was around 6:00 p.m., the time my dad got off of work. Because I was missing, she was late picking him up.

I was scolded and shuffled into the car to go pick my dad up. That is the last memory I have from that day, but the impact lasted for decades. For the next 15 years,

I kept the rape a secret. I never told anyone, not even my mother.

Fast forward 28 years, being raped at such a young age had a significant impact on my life, but this horrible incident also had purpose. Today, I have the honor of being able to share my story, my gift, with women like you! Maybe your story isn't like mine, or maybe you have a story that is worse. The fact remains that your story has an intended purpose; it happened for a reason! Coming into an understanding of why horrible things happen to us and understanding its purpose will help you overcome those things. This knowledge helped me overcome being raped.

I know how you feel. I know there have been moments where you feel like things are falling apart and wonder "Why me?" I felt the same way until I realized that all those moments were preparing me to be able to empower others. I understand being raped when I was younger only contributed to and enhanced the story I get to share with you. I can confidently say that I would not change anything that happened to me, including this rape. Be encouraged that bad things don't happen to defeat you or take you out. They happen because they were intended to show you that you are strong enough to bounce back from these things and grow to a place where you can help those who are not yet strong enough to bounce back. When the hits come, hit back and remind yourself that everything that happens to you has an intended purpose.

LIFE LESSON:

The things we experience in life are often allowed and even intended, not for our benefit but to inspire, encourage, and impact others.

Trials into Triumphs

by Veleda Spellman

I believe that all women possess special gifts that can continuously be unwrapped!

GIFT:
TRIUMPH

Have you ever felt so powerless at a point in your life that you wanted to give up? I know how you feel. I have often felt that way so much that I felt nothing and no one else mattered, not even living. I was under so much stress that I wanted an easy way out and did not care if I lived or died. During a tumultuous time in my life I allowed the way people viewed me and what they said have a severe impact on the way I thought.

My life was in such shambles that I felt there was nowhere to turn. The friends and family I thought were in my corner were the ones who were contributing to my emotional downward spiral. Are you the person who is always there for others, but help never seems to come when it's your turn? Are you the woman who loves hard but always get the short end of the stick when it comes to that same love reciprocating itself? This has happened to me numerous times. I was domestically abused, cheated on, and made to feel like my life was worth absolutely nothing. Suffering a broken nose, having plugs of my hair pulled out, and living in a tent on a campground because I wanted to be with that special someone and felt that was my way of being loyal. I suffered so much turmoil at the hands of men that I forgot what love was. I didn't even love myself!

My turning point was my husband leaving me to be with someone else. I begged and pleaded him not to go, but that was to no avail. After that, it seemed like the people who were supposed to be lifting me up were tearing me down. Those calling to console me were just gaining information to use against me. My relationship had spilled onto social media, which had become a tool used to publicly humiliate me and my relationship. What I thought to be a wonderful way to display my relationship in a good way had quickly become reminiscent to a nightmare. My significant other even joined in, telling much of our personal business online, using it to tear the very core of my soul. Our relationship was the laughing stock of many towns, and I was embarrassed to show my face anywhere. People were posting pictures and making memes. The fairytale was now a nightmare and my sunny days were now rain-filled. I felt like people had been praying for my downfall the whole time.

It was too much to bear, so I contemplated suicide. There was no need for me to exist anymore because I had put my life and trust in the hands of someone who did not have my best interest at heart. I began thinking of the pros and cons of committing suicide and decided to speak with my cousins Calvin Lynch Senior, Barbara, Calvin Junior and his fiancé Jessica. They were very instrumental in allowing me to see that life was worth living. If I did not have faith in God, I would have ended my life and let those seeking my downfall win.

I attribute my family for allowing me to see that your loved ones can and will be there for you in a time of need. I was able to regain my self-esteem by praying and keeping myself busy. Surrounding myself with certain friends and family while also attending church services was essential in my upward spiral. In order for me to achieve happiness, I had to make small positive changes in my life. When you surround yourself with negative people, places, and things, they erode the very core of your being. Everything starts with loving yourself and putting God first. You have to set time out during each day to allow your mind to breathe.

Also create a Me Time space, where you and God can go and have a team huddle. When you have a team huddle with God, you have created a game plan that no man can enter or break. I was fooling myself by thinking that happiness hinged upon my significant other, friends or family. I realized that unless my happiness came from within, I would constantly allow room for negativity to prevail in my life. After you have established a Me Time space (or huddle with God), you have to forgive that which has brought negativity in your life. Until you forgive, true healing cannot take place because you are becoming a slave to someone else. People will try to control you by projecting their negative energy to absorb your positive energy. Once I realized that it was necessary for healing, I was no longer a slave and they were no longer my prisoner. Harboring all those negative thoughts made me the epitome of negativity. I was negativity's poster child. I started to look for the positives among the negative in my life. See the sunshine among the clouds. I forced myself to exhale the negative and inhale the positive. It was time to move on and live my life, taking a stand against negativity.

We mistakenly think that change and being positive happens overnight. It's one thing to be a work in progress and another to be a piece of work in progress. I chose to be a work in progress, taking the necessary steps that I needed to become a Positive Queen. It was this ordeal that helped me start the group "Positive Queens." I felt that if social media was so powerful that it could make someone feel worthless, the same platform could be used to make someone feel priceless. This space was designed to house nothing but positive posts and inspiration.

I started Positive Queens in November of 2014 with a little over 200 women. We began sharing stories and current events with one another, then I decided to open up about why I started it. Once I did that, other women began expressing their problems and gratitude to me for giving them the courage to talk about their problems. I'd made it a positive support group where everyone could vent, bond, and create an internet sisterhood. When I started Positive Queens, I did not expect it to have such a domino effect in women's lives, even leading them to add other members.

In the beginning of January 2016, Positive Queens had close to 1,200 members. By the end of the same month we had catapulted to almost 10,000 women nationwide. The idea that women all over the world are going through domestic violence, cancer, loss of a loved one, and many other situations made me realize that there was a need for this group. There have been many situations that have arisen within the group that could have been catastrophic if women had no one to talk to. There was one instance where a woman was going to commit suicide and posted it on the page. Another woman saw it and alerted me immediately. After finding out her address, I was able to call the authorities and they showed up to her door before any harm could be done. Other women in the group near her area came to her home then followed the police to the hospital to sit with her.

Today, the group has over 90,000 women members.

It is amazing how friendships were built through the sharing of similar experiences. I realize that through my own trials and tribulations, I helped other women with theirs. Also women could help other women through shared experiences. So many women's lives have been touched and saved by this group. My life has a purpose of enabling other women to feel that they now have a purpose. I wake up every morning knowing that other people rely on me for motivation, inspiration, empowerment, and spiritual advice. Women can come to the page and not feel like they will be ridiculed or singled out because they are going through something. They are finding out that others are facing similar situations and are striving in the midst of their storm. Positive Queens gives meaning to those who feel meaningless and hope to those who are hopeless.

LIFE LESSON:

Your tests are your testimonies, trials are triumphs, and weaknesses strengths. Everything that you go through has a reason and a season. Every tear that you cry is only water that your life's flowers need to grow in your growth season. Do not let anyone make you feel like you are worthless, because you are priceless. "To help someone along the way is truly living, for it is humanity."

Do Away with Negative Thinking

by D.L. Jordan

I believe that we are born to be winners.

Have you ever looked back on part of your life and thought, "There is no way I can move forward? How can God restore my life? How can my present and future be used for greatness with a past like mine?" Before you were formed in your mother's womb, you were gifted and had purpose! Do you know that you were made to be triumphant and victorious?

Sadly, most of us do not believe that we are gifted, purposeful, or even worthy enough to be all that we can be. How we think and what we think, we become. The mind is like a lens that forms images of our thought process. The thoughts then allow brain chemicals to be released, making you aware of what it is you are thinking at that moment. If you think of something positive, great, or wonderful, your mind will burst with energy and imagine that great and wonderful thing. If you think of something negative, sad, or unconstructive, then your mind and body will react dolefully to those thoughts.

Thoughts are extremely powerful. What and how we think affects our mind, body, and soul. Thoughts can make our mind and body feel good or feel bad. Every cell and faction of our body is affected by our thoughts. If one gets emotionally upset, they begin to feel and have physical symptoms such as stomach aches and headaches. Positive and negative thinking is conceived in the mind and birthed through our speech. Whatever we think, positive or negative, we are planting a seed. Whatever we speak, we are watering that seed. How it is produced begins the growth process, and so will its harvest be. Keep in mind that your thoughts are not always truthful. Oftentimes your thoughts lie to you.

I recall a time in my life when I was going through a serious legal issue. In my heart and mind, I knew that I had done nothing wrong; my intentions were pure and innocent. I have always been a person of integrity and did things by the book. I began asking God, "Why am I going through this? I do not deserve what is happening in my life right now." Now, please understand that I am a believer in God. He knows me better than I know myself. If I had thought about who *I am* to Him first instead of dwelling on what was planned to happen to me, then I could have saved myself a lot of time, energy, and unwarranted thoughts. I positively channeled my thoughts and beliefs, and trusted God. I began reciting scriptures and passages from the Bible: *God will keep him in perfect peace whose mind is stayed on Him.* And that I did. I lifted myself out of my despoiled mire of thoughts where I was quickly sinking and just simply trusted God.

If you change your mind, you will change your world! If you think that you will not get that promotion, or believe that life will not get better for you, and feel that you cannot get yourself out of debt, then you won't. When you have a negative thought process that is in a whirlwind going around and around that are impervious to you, believing the truths of what and who you really are, you remain stuck in a place of pain, grief and unhappiness. Where does negative thinking stem from? It starts from what is seen or heard then becomes a course of action. First you hear or see something negative, then you wonder about it or reflect on it. As a result, you begin to express and voice the negative word or thought you saw or heard. Ultimately, the pessimistic attitude overtakes you and you begin to feel hopeless.

Perhaps something transpired in your past that causes you to feel less than or even worse. There may have been someone who repeatedly told you that you are incapable of achieving a goal or becoming someone great. I want you to know and understand that you were not born into this world to believe or be made to feel undeserving, hopeless, incompetent, or inadequate. YOU were born to be a winner! YOU were born to be healthy! YOU were born to be a leader! YOU were born to be a success! YOU were created to be and believe that YOU are gifted and born with a purpose!

We simply cannot allow negative people or negative thinking to be a part of our circle. How we think and feel about ourselves is a reflection of how we perceive our inner person, our outer appearance, our present and future, and how we carry ourselves. Additionally, we allow our negative thoughts and beliefs and regards of others keep us from living our best life. We must not give power to negative thinking, whether coming from us or someone we know. We need not say what we see but say what we desire. It is solely up to you. YOU can choose to think good thoughts. You must learn how to change, challenge, and correct your thoughts and start creating a new way of thinking and speaking to make your life better.

In my book, *Living Life Like It's Golden...The Latter Years of My Life Shall Be the BEST Years of My Life,* I mentioned that I had taken a day off from work to sort of sit in the quiet and get to know who I really was, why my life was going the way it was and why was I thinking so negatively about myself. Negative thoughts had enveloped and become a part of me and I had to figure out a way to totally do away with thinking negatively and not have it in my thought space. I had just come out of a marriage that ended very salty. I was not sure on how I could move forward or how I was going to take care of my two young children and handle my monthly expenses. First, I asked God to help me in this situation. Then I had to get my thought pattern together because I knew that in order for things to change in my life, I had to challenge and change my thoughts. I learned that if I speak positivity to myself and in my life consistently, I will begin to believe my words. Negative words also have that same effect. This is why it is so important to speak life and not death in to your life.

Women, in particular, are so apt to thinking negatively of themselves and do not make time to fully understand and believe who we really are. If something goes wrong, we begin to doubt who we are, develop feelings of depression and dejection, which leads to thoughts and beliefs of hopelessness, and feelings of worthlessness. But I want to let the world know that you, I, and women in general are resilient, amazing, unstoppable and STRONG! This is why I want all women to create and repeat over and over again a positive and encouraging mantra or phrase that would help elevate, promote, and uplift us on a daily basis. And by making this act a habit, we will be very surprised at how our inner and outer self will begin showing signs of self-love and improvement.

I make it a habit to encourage myself daily. And why do I do this? I do this because negativity lurks and seeks a place of refuge and comes in many forms. Therefore, it is important to secure myself against any negative mental attacks that may come my way. There are a few encouraging declarations that I recite often. One is about the importance of transforming your mind and the way we think by Chris Oyakhilome from his book, *The Power of Your Mind*: "It's your responsibility to transport yourself from one level of glory to another in your life. You can live a better and more glorious life by your choice, and he (God) has shown you here exactly how to do it—by renewing (effectively managing) your mind." The other is from Proverbs 23:7, "For as he thinks in his heart, so is he…"

Through regular reinforcement, I *began* and continue believing that I am a powerful individual and that I am truly God's masterpiece. And you should too!

LIFE LESSON:

Always believe that you are somebody! Always believe that you are an achiever! Always believe that you can be anything you put your mind to! Always believe in the impossible! Always believe that you are a person of greatness! Remember that you are a gift and that you are gifted. Do not allow negative thinking to control you and let life pass you by because you did not feel worthy enough to open your package. You are meant to be awesome.

My Next Awakening

by Ca Bap

I believe that no one can put a time limit on your life.

They said there was nothing else they could do. They told me to just live my life. I didn't know what to think. I was preparing to die.

I came home from work at 8 p.m. Eight hours later, my life changed forever. I had my first grand mal seizure. The sky was still black as I was rushed to the hospital in the wee hours of the morning. Doctors reported that I had two tumors on the left frontal area of my brain.

The seizures continued. I fell off the bed in the emergency room. With two black eyes and a hematoma on the front of my forehead, which can be likened to an extremely large bruise, I looked like I had been in a boxing match and lost, bad. I didn't look like the beautiful bride who got married on the sandy beaches of the Bahamas just one year before. I continued seeing neurologists and brain surgeons for the next three months. They finally made a decision to operate and remove the tumor. The date was set for surgery. I now know what it means to surrender. Anything of material value—money, jobs, and business—did not matter. Wealth is nothing without good health.

My coworkers, who were like family, kept calling me at home. They were so angry and upset that I was sick. I knew they were just scared, but I had made my peace. I had to remain calm for them and for myself. Sometimes, I forgot who was sick. Me or them? I asked them not to be angry and to pray for me. The night before surgery, my Great Spirit and I were conversing. The conversation ended with, "I trust and believe. Thank you!" Ten minutes before midnight, my phone rang. It was the surgeon saying he could not perform the surgery. A dear friend of his passed away and he had to go out of town. He explained that he could perform the surgery, but he preferred to be around for the follow-up and he would be unable. He recommended another surgeon, just as qualified as him, who I went to see a month later. I took several tests and another MRI. During my visit to the new doctor, he said to me, "I don't know what this is."

I was in shock and didn't know what to say. From his experience, the surgeon thought he saw two blood vessels.

One left a scar and the other absorbed itself. That's what causes the seizures. There were other things, but he did not have a definitive answer. When I left his office, I felt like a zombie. "What is going on? Can someone please explain what's wrong with me?" were the thoughts silently screaming in my mind.

I went to see my neurologist and told him what the other doctor had said. He replied that there was nothing more he could do and that I would be on medication for the rest of my life. He advised me to live the best life I could and bid me farewell. Well, what do you say to that?

THE DESTINY BEGINS

Five years prior to my first seizure, a dark spot the size of a freckle appeared beneath my bottom lip. It wouldn't go away. I went to several doctors, but no one could tell me what it was. After several biopsies, the discoloration stretched into a quarter-sized spot, permanently scarring my face. I accepted my new look and continued searching for answers. After four and a half years, I was finally diagnosed with discoid lupus. Though the disease had laid dormant for over 25 years, I had always been extremely sensitive to sunlight.

Sensitivity to the sun is one of the symptoms of lupus and manifests as swarms of little bumps when over exposure occurs. During a vacation to the Bahamas with my then fiancé, we took a water taxi to another part of the island. The taxi was a double decker and my husband wanted to sit out on the open air level. I wanted him to see what happens to me when I'm in direct sunlight for too long so there'd be no secrets between us before we got married. After a few minutes in the sun, I could feel my skin beginning to tingle. One by one, the bumps started to rise. He was shocked. I grabbed my things and ran down to the first floor where I would be protected from the sun.

Lupus is a disease in which the body's immune system mistakenly attacks healthy tissue. It can affect the skin, joints, kidney, brain, and other organs. Over time, my discoid lupus diagnosis turned into systemic lupus. Living with lupus can be painful at times, but I don't let this stop me from living. I must keep moving. I never returned to work as I was deemed too much of a risk. I was placed on sick leave and eventually retired. My coworkers held a fundraiser to help with my medical expenses for the next six months.

The cost of living in New York became too overwhelming, so I decided to move to Georgia. I was extremely sick and depressed for the first three years. My seizures were still not under control and I continued to have lupus flare-ups. In my mind, I was preparing for death. I went to a cemetery, bought a plot, and prepared for my demise. During this time, I also suffered a lupus-related stroke. My short-term memory, speech, and sense of balance all took a hit.

One day in meditation, my Great Spirit and I had a talk. I said, "I don't want to feel this way anymore." That was the beginning of my mindset change. I remember the doctors telling me there was nothing else they could do. At that point, I had another idea. I took one day at a time, giving thanks for each day. My challenges still exist, but I look at life with a different pair of eyes. No one can put a time limit on your life. When it's your time to expire, there is nothing you can do.

Sixteen years later, I'm still here, living my life to the fullest and enjoying everything my Great Spirit created. I stand before you as a retired locomotive engineer who was the second African-American woman to hold such a position in the history of that company. Since then, I have been a mentor, inspiring women to do their best and motivating them to step out of their comfort zone and face their fears (false emotions appearing real).

When I'm not feeling well, I take time to rest and rejuvenate. After years of trying to improve my skin's condition from discoid lupus, I discovered a natural way to treat my skin—a body butter that works wonders. My team of shea chefs formulated a natural skin moisturizer called Fab 222 Body Butter Crème that makes my skin radiant and soft.

I was diagnosed in 2000, and it took me two years to change my mindset. I found grace in the midst of despair, and despite what doctors told me, I have lived a long and fruitful life. I love to travel, try new things, and meet interesting people. Life isn't promised to anyone. Live your life to the fullest!

LIFE LESSON:

Find peace, grace, and happiness in all aspects of your life.

Sweet from Sour:
Saved by a Supermodel

by Ms. Candy Blog

I believe everything happens for a reason.

GIFT:
TRIUMPH

It pains me to say it, but I've been depressed for as long as I can remember. And I feel such sadness and shame to write that. At about seven years old, I remember asking my mother what to do if I was sad. "Think of nice and pretty things like lollipops or merry-go-rounds," she said. Somehow that didn't fix it. I'm pretty sure my first suicide attempt was my sophomore year of high school. I distinctly remember alluding to killing myself in a poem I wrote. My parents never took me to a doctor. Given my behavior, you would think they would've taken me to a doctor.

I was threatened that I would end up on lithium and to stop acting like (insert name of relative with mental illness). That should've been the clue. There were others in the gene pool who suffered from mental illness, so why wasn't I taken to a doctor and helped? Instead, I suffered until after college when I was on my own and took myself to a doctor. A cousin of mine who was mentally ill said, as she was dying from breast cancer, that the pain from cancer was one thing, but the depression was worse.

I have fought so many battles with myself to just go forward, to just do at least one thing to try and pull myself from the quicksand. I feel like I'm drowning and can't stop falling under and in. And I have to pull myself up. My depression has cost me friendships, relationships, and jobs. You have to postpone, cancel, or quit rather than explaining the truth because…well, that would be embarrassing. So you have two options: 1. Be honest, weird, and most likely stigmatized, or 2. Hide the truth and get pigeonholed as a bummer, buzzkill, and quitter.

Fun, right? Welcome to depression: the part you probably didn't know about. I guess "normal" people wake up and go to work or school. For me, though, it's a battle. I'm a worker; don't get it confused. I can sit and work all day long, but I can't get up and leave the house and be normal. Normal people don't burst into tears at will. Depressed ones do. I've been on pretty much every medication out there, mixing them with this one or that one, taking this one in the a.m. and that one right before bed.

I've been called a high functioning manic depressive with depression, which accounts for the amount of work

I'm able to accomplish and my creativity. Apparently, creatives are typically manic depressives—Robin Williams and Jim Carrey are the two I always refer to, as I think their work is genius. The Michael Keaton film, *The Birdman*, is about its main character's bipolarity. It didn't strike me as odd at all. With two theatre degrees to my name, I just figured that's how all theatre people behaved.

Ah, theatre! The place where all lost souls converge! Theatre lets us hide behind the masks of comedy and tragedy, and so many tragic stories are behind those masks that free us from the chains of whatever organized way of thinking has bound you—society, religion, family, relationship, etc. During my time in the theatre, RuPaul's "Supermodel (Of the World)" was released. The music became the soundtrack to my life. The album art—a part of one project I created—RuPaul, and drag became the inspiration behind a character I created in a show. Let it be said: A drag queen saved my life.

In mid-2013, I found myself without a job. The job wasn't right for me and I was very depressed about it. I was on a constant drip of RuPaul's *Glamazon* album as I diligently searched for a job, crying all day and night, wishing something would happen. Then one day, in the winter of 2014, something did.

I decided to create something that would bring me happiness, which in turn would bring happiness to other people. I thought, "Okay, I'll start a blog." *But what would it be about?* I thought, "Well, I like fashion and beauty." *But there are a million fashion and beauty blogs.* I also considered that it should be about something I'd like and want to write about for a very long time.

For as long as I can remember, candy has played a role in my life. Whenever my brother, sister, or I walk into a store that sells candy, the candy aisle is the first place we visit. An analysis occurs: what's new, what's been rebranded, what's been resized or is being offered in a different size, is the seasonal candy on the shelf yet--why or why not, but most importantly, WHEN? I might add that my husband, too, does all of these scientific examinations (and that was prior to meeting me)!

So I figured, "Well, candy shows up in fashion and beauty a lot. I'll focus on candy, but for a fashion and beauty loving audience." And then, as I'd learned in costume and scenic design, I began creating concept boards of how I wanted the brand/blog to look. Fonts from fashion magazines and fashion illustrations came together with the store design of Victoria's Secret (black and white stripes with plush hot pink furniture). My husband designed the logo and blog design, which uses Vogue magazine's font and features rainbow stripes, as candy is bright and multicolored. How's that for candy and fashion? Then there's the tagline: "Where candy is always in vogue!"

But the name! That was perhaps the hardest part. It had to have "candy" in it so those searching for "candy" would easily find it, and it was going to be a blog so....

Originally, it was going to be "Candy Blog, Sugar," to be read with a pause before the "sugar" as if said in a sassy tone with a snap! Then while talking to my husband about *RuPaul's Drag Race*, Ms. Candy Blog was realized.

In May 2014, RuPaul released a candy bar! (WHAT?! I'm creating a candy blog inspired by RuPaul, and RuPaul has a candy bar?! Was this written in the stars or just a strange coincidence? Oh my gawd!) At the same time, I went to the largest gathering of confectionary in the US, the Sweets and Snacks Expo, and pitched Ms. Candy Blog to the candy industry. Companies were receptive and gave me a lot of candy—a suitcase full!

June came and I finally found employment at YouTube of all places. How could I work at YouTube with Ms. Candy Blog in my back pocket and not have a YouTube channel? I shot videos of all of the candy I brought home, plus the RuPaul candy bar. I uploaded the first video (the RuPaul one) on a Monday, and that Friday, World of Wonder, the production company of *RuPaul's Drag Race* contacted me with an offer to join their YouTube network.

I spent the next year and a half creating candy and RuPaul focused videos for YouTube before discovering livestreaming, where the audience interacts in the moment of the live video. I have a performance background, so I thrive off the energy created by the viewers entering the room, their thoughts, and the stream of emoticons. It is this very energy that gave rise to the true character of Ms. Candy Blog.

Prior to shooting my YouTube videos in mid-2014, I had a sense of what I wanted Ms. Candy Blog to be—and yes, I often differentiated between me and "her," which drove my husband nuts. "She is you," he used to say, but I didn't think so. It wasn't until livestreaming that I came to understand that Ms. Candy Blog is the drag version of me—larger than life, quick, and sassy. She's not worried about what other people think, and she does and says what she pleases.

She also gets away with some pretty bold makeup and clothing. While YouTube/livestreaming performances are delivered in a black Ms. Candy Blog t-shirt topped off with a big, bon bon headpiece, in-person appearances require candy couture. I've curated a collection of candy influenced clothing, while also creating a few pieces on my own as worn at the RuPaul's Drag Con 2016. I even partnered with CandyJar.com to share the very candy, which inspired my fashion, bringing happiness to those I met in person at the convention!

It's been two years since the inception of Ms. Candy Blog. I still wrestle with depression and some days are much worse than others, but there's always Ms. Candy Blog, which, I've been told by a number of people, is a source of inspiration and joy. RuPaul and I met at his first Drag Con, where I thanked him for saving my life, and I received a warm reception from him at his second Drag

Con. You can learn more about both experiences on my YouTube channel.

Candy kisses!

LIFE LESSON:

"When you become the image of your own imagination, it's the most powerful thing you could ever do." — RuPaul

---

Mommy Issues:
Toxic to Triumph

by April Butcher

I believe your purpose creates prosperity.

I want to share the greatest triumph of my life. A lot of women have daddy issues, but there is one issue that a lot of us have in common but rarely speak about: mommy issues.

My parents wedded very young. My dad was 19 and my mom 14. They grew up living directly next door to each other. Once married, they lived with my dad's mom. Shortly after, I arrived. They also had a very active social life, so I lived with Grandmother for years, even after my parents were established. I grew very attached to my grandmother during this time. So attached that I never saw my life past her front door.

When I was 14, she passed away and her house was up for sale within a week. The life I had planned with her had ended. No matter what our plans are in life, God has a different plan set. After the passing of my grandmother, my brother and I went to live with our parents. I was so depressed during this time. I didn't like my mother at all because I felt she didn't love me. As children we only see a one-dimensional view of a person and we don't understand the complexity of life.

I felt my mom hated the one person who loved me, my grandmother. It came across as if my mom would stop at nothing to stomp my fire out. She would verbally and physically diminish my being. I was called stupid so many times, I thought stupid was my name. Some people hate because of the love others have for you.

While living with my mom, we attended a Pentecostal church. For those of you who aren't familiar with this religion, you are told as a female that you are not allowed to wear makeup, jewelry, and pants. The "holiness" upbringing left me embarrassed and broken because of the lack of acceptance from my peers.

The pressure from being ridiculed at school and coming home to a mother who seemed to not care about me at all was too much. One evening after being yelled at and beat, I said I had enough. Since she didn't love me, I'd go to someone who did. I sat on my mom's restroom floor and took a whole bottle of aspirin, which I'm allergic to, and waited to die. As I drifted off, I remember feeling scared, but relieved at the same time.

Again, God always has a plan set and is always in control. When I woke, I questioned how this could be. *Why am I still here?* But I knew in that moment God said He was not ready for me yet. As time went on, I grew to envy the relationship between my mom and my brother. They always seemed to be so happy. He's always seemed to have her support throughout life while I yearned for that feeling of acceptance. I also envied my mother's friendships and her attention to their needs, their wants, and how she would always look out for their best interest. I also saw, however, how they would mistreat her and let her down when she needed them most. I wanted my mom to be proud of me, to give me the love I so desired. I wanted to show her that she could love me and I wouldn't leave her like everyone else.

Yet, there is something we each have to realize about people. If an individual is not equipped with the tools to give you the two things that you need—love and acceptance—love them enough to let them go. I wanted love and acceptance. Some of the same things I required of my mom, she required herself. Though she didn't ask, her actions spoke volumes in her interactions with her siblings, spouse, and kids. I go back to an old song by Foreigner titled, "I Want to Know What Love Is." I think about one line that says, "I want you to show me." Some people have to be taught.

As time went on I learned that these experiences left

scars. I began acting out in school and failed tremendously. When I didn't graduate high school, my mom shipped me off to Houston, Texas to live with her sisters. I felt so alone, even though I was with family. My first week living in Houston, my aunt lost power due to a major ice storm. For two days in an ice cold house without lights, I felt my parents had forsaken me. I couldn't see the things that I'd done to contribute to this disconnect, just my pain.

The one thing that kept me motivated was my hope of making my parents proud so I could move back home. I worked extremely hard and graduated from high school. My parents were excited and overjoyed that I was going on to college. I moved back home to begin the next level, but this was only a temporary bandage. I majored in Performing Arts at the University of Southwestern Louisiana.

My dancing was my outlet. I made the cut for an elite performance called State of LA Danse. When I returned home to share this major accomplishment, no one cheered. I was devastated! I thought, "Don't they know how important this is?" This broke me. I realized, good would never be good enough. I dropped out of college and drowned myself in work and partying. Year after year, it was up and down between us. Arguments, shouting matches, and slammed doors. *How could the closest thing to me hate me so much?* What I didn't know was that she felt the same.

By the time I turned 23, my mom had her third child and I was in LOVE! I consumed myself in my baby brother. He was my new love—someone I could love who would love me back. I would tote him everywhere with me. I eventually went back to school to study radiology, and I'd take him with me there too. It was rough not having support. Lonely too. My relationship with my mother never improved; it got worse. And I went from drowning myself in work and partying to school and God. I got closer to Him just to keep my sanity. For years, my scars got worse because of the friendships I encountered. Following the patterns of my mom, I gave without receiving and let friends take precedence just to feel some form of acceptance. I poisoned myself with toxic relationships that left me drained and my storage empty.

I graduated radiology school in August of 2006 and begin working in my field. I met my boyfriend in December of 2006 and instantly fell in love. I knew from the moment we met that he would be my strength to lean on. March of 2007, I made the decision to move out of my parents' home and never return. I found love, peace, and protection in my boyfriend Brian. We were engaged in June and married April of 2008. My mom and dad refused to pay for our wedding, but when you're in the will of God, no one can stop his Divine Order. We worked hard to make money to pay for the wedding. With just three months to plan and pay, our wedding was paid in full. That was truly the power of God.

Seven years later, my daughter Madison was born. I thought things would get better after having her, but (as always) it didn't. Going through post-postpartum was a nightmare, and I needed my mom most. I begin seriously praying to God for change, a resolution. In March of 2016, PERIUNION™ changed everything. I never thought planning this event would impact my life in such a profound way. Let me explain.

At the age of 21, my mom was a savvy entrepreneur. She owned a successful beauty salon for 19 years. She prided herself on having her own salon because she only has a 10th grade education. When I first started planning the global gathering of social media influencers called PERIUNION™, my mom didn't believe or know what exactly I was working towards. Once the event was completed, my mom heard the testimonials and saw the results. She was overjoyed to see my accomplishments and could finally be at peace with her plans for my life, knowing I had accomplished what was, in her mind, a level of success.

Since March, our relationship has grown leaps and bounds. Sometimes our parents love us so hard, it smothers us in growth. You know, people express love differently, and they don't always know how to get their message across. My mom wanted me to be great but could only display the road to greatness in discipline. One thing about my life experiences is that I don't regret one. I have forgiven my mother. And in granting forgiveness, you find peace that passes all understanding. For with forgiveness you can move forward and above.

Each trial has made me wiser. Each scar has made me stronger. Never allow anyone to steal your fire. Like a locomotive needs coal to fuel its momentum, you need just one person, one scripture, to fuel your fire to greatness. So many women never make amends with their moms. I am so fortunate I did. My story of triumph may seem small to others, but a mother's love can move mountains. This my story.

LIFE LESSON:

I have learned in life that acknowledging your contributions to life's dysfunction allows you to then be triumphant.

Losing Everything Helped Me Find My Purpose

by Tanisha Mackin

I believe that all things happen for a reason.

We may not understand the reason for the things that happen to us, but they are learning experiences for us to grow. For years, I tried figuring out my purpose in life. I ventured out into several businesses that did not succeed, but were great learning experiences. In 2010, I thought I figured out my calling when I was diagnosed with stage 2 colon cancer. This news hit my family hard as I thought I was going to lose my life.

But I decided to fight and not give up. During chemotherapy, I decided to go back to school for my MBA in Healthcare Management, a field I was determined to get into after being sick myself. I wanted to assist patients with their financial accounts, finding assistance if they couldn't pay for care, and just being a helping hand in special programs associated with cancer patients. During my four hours of treatment, I would do online classes and receive encouragement from the doctors and nurses who cared for me.

The feeling of finally finding my calling was so overwhelming and exciting. My husband, who I married prior to starting my classes and being diagnosed with colon cancer, was very proud of me. Note: We married on August 14, 2009. My husband was my backbone and very protective of me. He helped me in any way possible while I was sick and caring for our newborn. I know this is what husbands are supposed to do, but we were 30 years young. Most guys would have left, I'm sure.

I felt like I could do anything in this world as long as we were together. But money was tight, because I went from being on maternity leave to medical leave from work. My paycheck decreased to nothing over time. He worked extremely hard to keep a roof over our heads and food on the table, while I attended school full-time and completed chemotherapy. It may sound crazy to you, but the time I had cancer was one of the best moments in my life. No, I didn't want cancer nor do I want it again, but the way we pulled together as a family during was amazing. I knew our family would be okay.

My husband and I were married in a Texas courthouse. No friends, no family, no rings, just the judge and two people who were madly in love with each other. Because of this, our family decided that we should do a wedding reception in our hometown of Buffalo, NY on our one-year anniversary. We were very excited as our family helped plan this event. I brought a nice wedding gown and my husband had a custom made suit. This would be the first time everyone had seen us since we were married, since being diagnosed with colon cancer, and having our second baby.

We had our weekend planned, but first we decided to hang out with family and friends who came in from all over to celebrate with us. We went to an upscale night club and hung out Friday evening. We were having a great time when the clock struck 12 a.m., officially making it our anniversary. While celebrating, we noticed commotion on the dance floor. Finally, the DJ stopped the music and told everyone to leave. As my husband and I walked to our car, we heard gunfire. No one knew where it was coming from, but it was extremely close. Somehow, I got separated from my husband and managed to get back into the nightclub. I stood by the door in fear as I watched my husband laying on the ground taking cover. All I remember hearing is gunshots and screaming.

Once the shooting stopped, I looked out the door and saw him get up and dust himself off. I was so relieved to see that he was okay, but then I noticed a red spot on his yellow shirt by his shoulder getting bigger and bigger. *Oh my God, my husband's been shot!* Once I got reconnected with my family, I told them that Dee (my husband) was shot. They finally unlocked the doors of the nightclub and I ran outside. I got outside in time to hold my husband and watch him take his last breath.

I remember laying on the ground next to him, cuddled up under him as if we were in our bed at home watching television. I completely shut down, and it didn't hit me that my husband, best friend, the father of my children, and the man I'd been with for 10 years was gone. I became a wife and a widow in exactly one year. A total of eight people were shot. Four were fatal, including my husband and a female friend I grew up with. "What do I do now?" I remember asking myself.

I was completely lost. I had two children, no job, no father for my children, and I was still battling cancer. I felt so alone. He was my best friend, lover, and definitely my protector. How was I going to return to our home in Austin, TX without him? While in Buffalo, I had to bury my husband in the suit that was intended for our wedding reception. I also had to deal with court and the DAs, but the outpour of love and support was overwhelming. People from all over sent money, milk, diapers, and school clothes and supplies for my children. I was very grateful for these things, as I didn't know which way to go in life. I knew I had to get healthy, I knew my son had to go to school, and I knew I had a baby to take care of, but at that point, I didn't care! I wanted to die so I could be reunited with him. There I was, a widow at

31 years old, a single mother of two amazing children, battling colon cancer, and a victim of violence. Life truly sucked for me.

Victim? After a few months of being in the bed, not caring about the outside world, I prayed to God to please take this pain off of me. The heartache hurt so bad that I thought I was going to have a heart attack, then I remembered that I had two children depending on me. I was their ONLY biological parent left.

I also decided that I wanted to do something for everyone who sent money, gifts, cards, text messages, and encouraging words, but I knew it was impossible to reach all those people. After speaking with my father, we started the Mackin Project in honor of my husband and to give back to the community. The Mackin Project is a non-profit organization designed to help widows and children who've lost a spouse or parent to violence. I wanted to help others like my children and myself, seeing as how when I became a widow I felt like I had no one to turn to.

I took some courses to become a certified bereavement coach to help other widows, through the five stages of grief. I felt like I found my purpose, but not fully; something was still missing. I wanted to get my story out there, as well as encourage others because I felt like, if I went through having a baby, colon cancer, and losing my husband within eight months and was still standing, I knew others could too. My mission in life is to help others and share my testimony. And I have done so, with my love of writing and creating a platform for other people to get their stories heard through writing, including a series of books I wrote to help widows and others who may be going through life-changing issues.

Helping others is my goal and passion. Today the Mackin Project has helped several families within the U.S. We offer care packages and bereavement coaching to widows and their families. I've written five books and I am a 2x bestselling author. I was awarded 2016 Memoir of the Year for my book titled, *My Testimony*, and my son wrote a book entitled *Fatherless Son* to help other children who face the loss of a parent. And last but not least, I started a stationery line known as the Destiny Collection, designed to encourage you while you write or take notes. I found my purpose through pain and loss. I turned my trials into triumph.

LIFE LESSON:

Live every day to the fullest. Life is too short to not live to your full potential.

Don't Sit on Your Fabulous

by Faye Thompson

I believe that we only hurt ourselves by suppressing or belittling our fabulous.

I love whipping up drama-drenched gems for my readers, and they always want more. *When's the next book coming out, Faye? How long do I have to wait? Whaat? Come on, Faye, you gotta do better than that.* You want to know something? They're right. Some days I *can* do better. Other days I'm doing the best that I can.

As an author, sometimes fiction is mind boggling. On the flip side, as a reader, sometimes you want to know more about authors than the veneered laundry list of accomplishments on social media. You've read their books, but what's *their* story?

Can I be honest with you? Can I remove my mascara

and lipstick? Slip out of my heels and Spanx and pop out my hair extensions? Thanks. And how about my pearls? Can I take them off too?

Cool. It's time to tell my story. Not of my heroines—not Bronze's, Charisma's, or Sable's journey but mine. Faye Thompson's story. We have each been given a mission according to God's purpose. He's the author, and this story is mine. The good, the bad, and the ugly. Like it or not. It's mine.

Today I'm removing my mask and putting on my armor because life takes courage. Yes, I'm a writer, student of life, and God's girl. I'm also a survivor of bipolar depression. According to the National Alliance of Mental Illness, it is estimated that 1 in 25 Americans live with a serious mental illness such as schizophrenia, bipolar disorder, or major depression. An estimated 7.8 million African Americans are living with a mental illness. For more information, go to: www. mental health.gov/get-help. If you are battling bipolar depression, I want you to know that you are not alone. We're in this together. It's not all in your head and you're not crazy. You have a disease, and you suffer in silence because the stigma is real. You sweep your condition under the rug like a dirty little secret for fear of rejection and being labeled crazy. You bottle it up. Maybe you self-medicate with alcohol, food, and compulsive shopping. *Girl, if my closets could talk.*

Your prayers are long and your conversation short. Other days your prayers are short and your conversation long. You put on a smile, and you wear it well. Inside, though, your soul is crying as you bury your pain. I know how you feel. I felt that way too. You backtrack. You beat yourself up and replay your past to pinpoint where you went wrong. Why me, Lord? You want anyone else's life but your own. If only you had done this or hadn't done that, maybe you would not have ended up here.

My *here* was the psychiatric ward three weeks after starting my freshman year in college. Imagine having to sign yourself out of the university of your dreams and on your birthday at that? It was without a doubt the lowest point in my life. The plan was becoming a plastic surgeon, but I missed the mark. Now what?

When you are going through a crisis, you feel disconnected. It's nobody's fault, however. Don't blame yourself. Mental illness is complicated, so seek professional help. My mother assured me that I could still be or do anything that I wanted to do. Even though she never made promises, she promised me that one day we'd look back at all this and laugh. "When we're dead?" I asked.

"No!" She insisted that we'd be sitting around the kitchen table and she'd say remember when…, then we'd bust out laughing. Weeks later during visiting hours, a nurse making rounds poked her head in the doorway. After she left, my mother asked me if I remembered what happened the day before, but I didn't. I had been squirming in my seat during visiting hours, but I was afraid that if I left to use the bathroom, my mother would be gone when I returned. So I sat and held it in. The nurse reminded me that if I didn't go to the bathroom, I would urinate on myself, to put it politely. I looked at her all nonchalant, shrugged one shoulder, and grunted. "So, I've done it before," I boasted. When my mother told me that story I laughed so hard that tears rain down my cheeks. I hadn't laughed in weeks, so it felt wonderful. Laughter truly is good for the soul. I was going to be okay. I made my mother retell that story every day for a week. Each time I laughed like the very first time. I was on my way to recovery.

You'd think I had learned my lesson and would never be hospitalized again, right? Wrong. A few years later I was admitted for a brief stay. My pastor spoke briefly with my mother. Decades later his words are still fresh in my mind. "Well, I think she's forgotten her first love." Time stood still. In that moment I realized that I belong. I belong to the family of God and we are united on a mission throughout eternity. My forefathers were depending on me to run my race, to be about my Father's business. I could almost hear them up in the bleachers cheering me on, moaning when I fell and rejoicing when I picked myself up, dusted myself off, and got back in the race.

You may feel like you'll never experience joy or happiness again. I felt that way too, but here's what I've learned: Mental illness is not a death sentence. It's God's way of pulling us over to the side of the road so He can take the wheel, so to speak. Mental illness affords us the opportunity to stop, reflect, recharge, regroup, and re-invent ourselves according to His plan. It's a reposition-ing. All of God's children have a cross to bear. We all have something. Mental illness is my something. I didn't choose to have a mental illness and neither did you choose the battle you struggle with, be it alcohol and drug addic-tion, fertility issues, raising a child with health challeng-es, post-traumatic stress disorder. We all struggle with or suffer from something. God doesn't make mistakes. We manage it. Therapy is a lifesaver. My grandmother often said that man's extremities are God's opportunities. Let God be God.

Learning to forgive myself was one of the hardest parts of my journey. We often treat others better than we treat ourselves. Forgive yourself for falling short of your own expectations. I expected to be a wife, a mother, and a plastic surgeon. God had other plans though. It is what it is. Instead of worrying about what's not in alignment with your expectations, take the time you need to get your life together. Every so often the clock on my night-stand stops at 11:59 p.m. Not 7:49 a.m. Not 11:59 a.m. Not 3:11 p.m. Always 11:59 p.m. Strange right? But maybe God wants to remind me who's in charge—not Mother Nature or Father Time. He is. He can speed time up or slow things down. He can even make time stand still. We have time.

You may think that God doesn't hear your cries, but He does. Remember how my 18th birthday was the lowest point in my life? Well, a few years ago I took a leap of faith to pursue writing full-time. The fact that my very first day of retirement happened to land on my birthday is a testament of God's love. He hooked up those dates just for me. God can bless you in such a way that there is no doubt in your mind that He is the source. He feels your pain and His timing is impeccable. He didn't bring you this far to say "Bye, Felecia." You were created for God's purpose, and you have a story to tell. Despite your diagnosis and current situation, you are blessed. Don't sit on your fabulous God-given gifts and talents. God is counting on you. Someone needs to know that they are not alone in their struggle.

Years ago I was traveling home with other out patients. The ambulette driver was rude, arrogant, and unfamiliar with the various neighborhoods on his route. A disabled woman with very limited verbal skills and I were the last two patients to be dropped off. We lived ten minutes apart. I prayed that she'd arrive home safely. The next morning, I requested a meeting with our social worker and complained about the driver. She informed me that it had taken him several hours to get the last patient home. Her mother was frantic.

The social worker requested a description of that driver because they were rotated daily. He was swiftly terminated. Later, she asked me why I had come forward. I told her that when you have a voice, you have to use it—especially when others can't use theirs. She thanked me from the bottom of my heart, like I was solving world peace.

People who love and respect you will continue to do so—before, during, and after you share your story. Those who don't won't, but don't despair. The fact that you are still breathing means you matter. You're relevant. You are purposed to be here and your mission is not complete. You have work to do, and because of what you have been through and are going through, you can help others. Let's open up a dialogue and remove the stigma of mental illness.

LIFE LESSON:

And we know that all things work together for good to those who love God, to those who are the called according to His purpose. (Romans 8:28) Even in your darkest hour, God's got you.

The Lies I Told Myself

by LaKita Stewart-Thomson

I believe that I am fearfully and wonderfully made.

I met one of my very best friends about 34 years ago. She came at a time in my life when I didn't really understand much. I was about three years old and we became really close. I trusted her with my life, and she later convinced me to write a letter to myself that I want to share with you.

It reads:

Dear the most unimportant person alive,

I absolutely hate you. You are the very reason your mother abandoned you and your father only tolerated you. You are the reason darkness even exists. The very presence of you is a foul stench in the nose of those who have to encounter you. The reflection you see when you look at yourself in the mirror is pure disgust. You are not or have never been important to anyone, especially not to yourself. You were a mistake and nothing you will ever do will be good enough. Take these razors blades and cut yourself until the blood drains completely out. If that doesn't work, take every prescription pill in the medicine cabinet until your heart explodes or your mind dissipates. If that doesn't work, get intoxicated or high and drive off a bridge and disappear. If that doesn't work, just run away as far as you can. No one will even notice you're gone. If that doesn't work, give yourself away to people who don't value you, who will abuse you and who will only take you for granted. If that doesn't work, just exist. Though you are alive, your inner soul is dead. Therefore, you have no earthly value. Take care of everybody else except yourself; you were really just an accident. Your imperfections are way too noticeable and nothing about your existence is worthy of you living. You are a waste and unimportant to yourself and everyone else. Your body, your mind, and your soul belong to me. You will never find a friend as good as me. Nobody sees you. Nobody hears you. Nobody wants you and nobody loves you. So why not die? Take your own life or be content just as unimportant as you were when you came into this world.

Signed,
Low Self-Worth

I love all that I am, just as I am ~ Unknown

As I reflect on the broken pieces of my past life, I can say loving myself was the most difficult thing for me to do for over 30 years. I allowed the pain of life experiences and disappointments to define my worth. I've allowed people's words, actions, and perceptions of me shape my view of who I was. I blamed myself for years for the rejection, for the sexual/mental abuse, neglect, and abandonment. I even sold my soul for acceptance and so-called love. My thoughts and emotions opened several doors in my mind and my life became meaningless.

I hid behind baggy clothes, shyness, work, and much insecurity. This is when depression set in and brought about mistrust, confusion, bitterness, anger, fear, and a strong lack of self-worth. Depression doesn't have a look. It doesn't discriminate. It's something we may not even realize we have. The symptoms aren't always noticeable; therefore, suicide was inevitable. I no longer wanted to bear the pain of being misunderstood, mistreated, and simply tolerated.

Just when I was about to throw in the towel, my prayer life became prevalent. Almost instantly, my life began taking a turn for the better. Though the road was rocky, the reward was great. It was a cold day in spring around 4:18 p.m. on March 21, 2008 when the sun shone through the clouds, the rain dried from the storm, and a rainbow appeared. In this moment, my heart transformed, a miracle appeared, and my healing process began. I discovered who I truly was, in the form of a little person.

God knew all about my troubles and He wrapped me in the cradle of His arms. He knew exactly what I needed and when I needed it. This is when I met my destiny and purpose in the form of a baby girl, full of love, joy, and life. This blessing inspired me to live and love without conditions. It took a little time to embrace her, but His love began illuminating through her.

The twinkle in her eyes gave me strength to live, and the power of God's love gave me desire to live. I believe God sent love in the form of a child to teach me all about His love, which has no conditions or end date. He sent the closest thing to Him to show me love as it should be. Initially, motherhood was quite faint to me. I felt abandoned and rejected for so many years and was in a world of my own for so long. Love was very vague and in my mind a hurtful thing. It looked like abuse, self-mutilation, sex, rejection, abandonment, alcohol, rape, and the list goes on. I did all these things to feel love that I could only get from knowing who I truly was in God. I couldn't give love or receive it, let alone love myself until I met my angel.

For the first time in life, I felt love with just a simple cry. Her name is Destinee, my purpose. Her presence caused me to do some soul searching. I searched long and hard and found a little girl within me needing to be embraced from the deeply driven scars on my heart—scars that I had to re-open in order to heal properly and with some realities. I wondered how I could mother when I didn't know mine. That was only the beginning.

As I found myself, God began revealing Himself in a mighty way and peeling back the layers of my heart so that I could love as He loves, despite my past. This road of self-discovery, self-love, and self-esteem was a rocky one, but there is hope for those who want to be better. My message to anyone reading this is that you are only defined by what you allow to define you. Your self-esteem, self-worth, and self-discovery are in knowing that you were created by God and He loves you more than anything. He created you before the foundation of the world and knew how to mold you and make you for His glory. He knew you before you were implanted in your mother's womb. You are fearfully and wonderfully made. His love is unfailing. Everything you endure is not for you but to help someone else. You are worth it. Your greatest hurts will come from those you love. On the other hand, your greatest success is a result of the very things that caused the most hurt and pain. Your experiences make you who you are and will drive you into your purpose. God will never give you something to great for you to handle. He will always provide a way, just seek him.

I never believed my heart could be completely healed. Though there are areas I am still working through, I am nowhere near where I was. I know that loving me is a must in order to love my baby and others. I know I am not the only one who suffered in the silence with loving me. We all wear various facades to hide who we really are. We all have at some point have gone without saying what we truly feel or think. We all have allowed some situation or person to dictate our self-worth. Well today is a new day and you can start by loving who you are first. It is the best thing you can do. Seek God and He will reveal to you who you are in Him.

LIFE LESSON:

Learning to love yourself will be the hardest thing you ever do, but it's possible.

Finally Finding Love

by Jennifer Hill

I believe that you accept the love you think you deserve.

I learned early and the hard way that love is never to be taken for granted. Our early relationships or environment creates our initial level of self-esteem. How we feel about ourselves determines how we relate to others. Each of these relationships, with ourselves and others, continually feeds the other. Going back and determining the root cause of any deficiency allows you to address it and move toward wholeness, self-acceptance, and self-love.

My grandfather was a wonderful surrogate. He was always clearly "Pops," but he was so good at it that I didn't realize what I was missing from my father until it became painfully obvious in my teenage years. He rarely returned my calls. I didn't have a phone number for him, so I'd have to leave messages with my grandparents. When we did connect, miscommunication, disappointment, and frustration were the norm. It was only a few months before his death that he gave me a number to reach him. I was an adult by then, and he had learned that my marriage became abusive. It was, for me, a sudden unexpected maturation. The final small but significant gesture came a few weeks before his death. We were sitting together amongst a small gathering celebrating the Fourth of July. While the festivities continued on around us, we quietly bonded.

I left my ex-husband and moved in with a man I had essentially just met. My family on my mother's side was resistant to taking me in for various reasons, including fear of violence following me, concerns about how much I could contribute to rent, how long I would stay, and whatever else they could come up with, leaving me feeling generally unloved. So I found it where I could. He was a decent guy and we ended up dating for a few more years after my son and I moved in with him, but not without complications.

Two months into my new living arrangement, I got pregnant. I could only attribute it to a late or missed dose of birth control. I was still legally married, fleeing from an abusive husband, trying to hold down a job, and most likely entering a custody battle for my then two-year-old son. I could only imagine the complications a pregnancy would add. I had no idea what my future would hold or if this new man would be a part of it. My heart and my head saw two different realities, and I realized how painful it is for a woman to be both pro-life and pro-choice at the same time.

I told him I was pregnant and of my decision to have an abortion. He was cold, detached, and had nothing to say. It was an emotionally challenging time for me without any support. Later in the relationship, I learned first through repeated micro-aggressions from his family, then finally a very telling sideways remark, that he had discussed my decision to have an abortion with his family, but never bothered discussing it with me. If he had just raised one word in objection, there's a very strong possibility I would now have another child. His making more of an effort to talk about me than to talk to me felt like a betrayal of epic proportion. I was tormented over the decision all over again.

When I first left him, my ex-husband would not let me take my son with me. Even though he had previously used our son as a pawn in his attempts to manipulate me, I knew he wouldn't hurt him if I was not around. I also suspected it wouldn't last. My maternal grandmother was my son's caretaker at the time. When my family realized my ex-husband was now taking advantage of the arrangement, leaving my son there for days on end, they put their foot down. Experiencing the challenges of single parenthood, my ex insisted I come get my son, and I was happy to oblige. After nine months of living with my boyfriend, my son and I were finally able to get our own apartment.

That small victory was short-lived. My father died of a

massive heart attack while sitting in the living room having a conversation with my grandfather, who died just a week and a half later having suffered from prostate cancer. When the two most prominent men in your life die ten days apart, it undoubtedly affects you (as if I didn't already have abandonment issues). I tried to be strong for my grandmother who lost both her husband and only child at the same time, but nothing will ever compare to the strength I drew from her at a time when she most needed support.

Understanding what you value in a relationship, striving to be that yourself, and accepting nothing less works wonders for your self-esteem. Before I got to that place, I made more mistakes and bad choices. I dated a married man, thinking I finally discovered what love was, despite the circumstances. I was so naïve. None of it was real. I realized that people aren't always who they say they are, and relationships that made me feel good were hard to come by. I learned to be more selective. Whether or not a man was someone I'd want my son to emulate further narrowed the field.

I acknowledged the typical probationary period for most employers and realized it was backed by science and had a broader application. I took more time to get to know people and I also started paying attention to how eager they were to actually get to know me. I applied that same 90-day probationary period to my relationships and realized just how real it was. I started seeing a clear pattern of men not surviving more than three months. The facades always fell away. Their interest in conversation became more important than VIP tickets. In reality, if a man is serious, he will want to spend just as much time qualifying or wanting to know everything about you as you do qualifying him. I would turn down invitations from probably great guys because their focus was in the wrong place: the vehicles they drove, references to their income, or other attractive women they had dated. I did not need the superficial validation of being desired. I wanted someone who was willing to go deeper; I wanted to be valued.

I met the next man I would get engaged to online. He lived across the state line, so getting to know each other before our first date was a given. When we met, we clicked, and it seemed like it was meant to be. We made plans to merge our lives and our families. We started off fast and furious, but when any part of you ever feels like the traffic flow is no longer evenly moving in both directions, then you have to pause, communicate and do your best to get things moving along again. Love is always a two-way street, and I tried. Gracefully exiting a relationship is just as important as making sure you are in the right one. And as proudly as I started recognizing my own worth, I tarnished that value in the way that I punctuated the ending of this one.

When you can openly acknowledge to yourself that what you are about to do—betraying the trust—essentially signifies the end of your relationship. Regardless of what you might discover, you've reached an amazing level of self-awareness and responsibility. It becomes way less amazing when you pick up his cell phone and check it anyway. I knew our relationship was over, I just needed to prove it to myself. I had never checked his phone before, so he had no reason to put it away or delete his activity. He had an explanation; he always did. It would have been so much easier if he had just confessed. I wish I had had the courage to take the responsibility for appropriately ending our relationship squarely upon my own shoulders, but I did not. Instead I gave him an impossible ultimatum, one that I knew he could never accept, that I am sure hurt him, although that was never my intent.

LIFE LESSON:

Learning to love yourself is hard enough, but when you've had a history of not getting the love you need as so many of us have, it's no surprise that many women never really learn to truly love themselves. My failed engagement was my last serious relationship for a long time. I did not anticipate the amount of time it would require to fully heal, but I recognized more than ever that I needed to work on me. The self-care practices that I learned over that time taught me so much about myself and overcoming my struggles with identity, abandonment, and self-love. I am still a work in progress, as we all are, but so proud of where I am now.

Love Just Is, Thy Will Be Done

by After Chloe

I believe without a doubt that love just is, thy will be done.

I don't remember ever being separated from my mother. Really, in my 34 years of life, I had never not talked to my mother at least 20 times a day. She was a super human, she was brilliant, had the faith of 20 deacons in a Baptist church, and was my best friend.

My memories of my mother include her laugh, her smile, and a very specific talk that she had with me throughout my life, constantly reminding me "love just is, thy will be done." She loved everyone and everything she encountered, but never had expectation. I, on the opposite end, had been married twice by the age of 34 and was getting ready to marry the third love of my life, but as my mama stated he was different.

She and my dad loved me so much no one else's love could compare. My parents never gave up on me—in spite of my drug addiction, mental illness, divorces, and my inability to truly value my life. Instead, they would always say, "Love just is, thy will be done."

In April of 2010, my mother had a massive heart attack and my father called me to go to be with them, which is the last time the three of us were together. My mother survived, but on June 27, 2010 my father went to the restroom and passed away of a heart attack. Seeing my mother so bewildered and heart broken, I felt so much pain. She waited for me and the love of my life to arrive. When we did, she had another massive heart attack. Again, she survived, but this time there was a part of her missing. I would often remind her that love just is, thy will be done, *right*? She would look far past me and I understood her pain overpowered her love; she hadn't been without my dad for over 47 years.

The third week of August in 2010 brought the news that I was expecting my first baby. I was scared and excited that the third love of my life, who was in fact different, was going to be the father of my only child. The pregnancy was stressful and all the while, Mama was getting worse day by day. Not so much for the cardiac issues physically, but instead a broken heart. I missed my parents so much and here I was having my first child, who was born on December 29, 2010 prematurely. Instantly, I understood exactly what "love just is, thy will be done" meant. I fell in love, love like I had with my parents. I watched the medical team save her life and take her to another hospital where there was NICU and where my daughter Chloe began fighting for her life.

Let's go back to "love just is, thy will be done." Love just is and regardless of what we want, God's prevails. I didn't completely understand that until the moment I saw Chloe. She fought for her life for over 60 days before passing away. The pain overtook me, I became crazed, and I wanted my life to end. Actually, my life did end. The whole time my mom was there, she kept telling me "love just is, thy will be done." And I would become so angry every time she said it. Life continued, but I was broken, shattered, and lost. My mother's condition continuously worsened, but I believed that God would not take the only person I had left. *How wrong I was?* On October 14, 2012, a little over a year and a half after Chloe passed away, my mom died. Prior to her passing, she was so worried what would happen to me and she kept repeating her favorite phrase. I wasn't angry anymore though. I was sad. I'd lost my ace, my everything.

Over the next few months, I contemplated suicide. I constantly felt a physical pain and seemed to cry nonstop. I woke up one day and her phrase came to mind again. I started to yell out, "What does that even mean?" Then I realized, once again, that regardless of losing what you cannot replace and losing yourself in the process is dangerous, the love that remains just is. Regardless of what I want, regardless of what I think should happen, it's God's will that will be. It's not for me to understand; it's for me to demonstrate that love will remain. As mama said, "Love just is, thy will be done."

I wish I could end this chapter with a happily ever after, but that wouldn't be the truth. What I can say is that the chapter isn't an end. It's been a beginning to understanding that when you lose what isn't replaceable, you will grieve and you will feel like you cannot go on, but I am here to remind you that love just is and God's will is for you to live life. Find your way to grieve. If you give up today, then start again tomorrow. You are worth it. You are worth an amazing life.

I don't think that I will ever get over losing my parents and my daughter, but I do know that I have gotten through the pain and that I am meant to serve others by sharing my journey. Making others realize that love just is, thy will be done applies in all facets of loss. Loss will stunt and disable but not destroy. That doesn't mean that I like it, but I have accepted it and I can share with you that I am happy most days living with Chloe's dad, my two dogs, and my mom's cat while helping those heal from losing what cannot be replaced.

LIFE LESSON:

Loving yourself is to get through the hard, impossible times. Loving yourself is knowing that the pain of loss is not permanent but a builder of strength. You've got this. Love just is, thy will be done. Remember that.

Corporate World Crash Down

by Sherie Wells

**I believe that every less than desirable experience
has a more than desirable outcome when it is used
as an opportunity for self-discovery and growth.
Through growth comes self-love.**

GIFT:
SELF-LOVE

Have you ever wondered who am I, what am I supposed
to be doing in this life, what direction do I go now?
Some days we believe we know exactly who we are and
where we are headed, and then, in an instant, everything
changes. Your identity, the person who you thought you
were, the person you prided yourself on being for years
is no longer who you are anymore. This happened to me
three years ago. One moment changed everything I knew
about myself. I no longer knew who I was anymore or
where I was headed. The confident person that I was no
longer existed.

Four years ago, life was going my way. I was happily married with three great kids, a roof over my head, a corporate job as a multi-unit manager with great pay, good benefits, and a company car. I was exceeding the company's expectations on a consistent basis, which led to big fat bonus checks every month, and I had a team of managers who respected me. We were killing it!

Everything was going smoothly, so my husband and I decided it was time to have another baby. This time we hoped for a girl. We already had one girl and two boys, so to be blessed with another girl to even out the numbers would be perfect! A month or so after we made the decision, we found out we were pregnant and were beyond excited. I was on cloud nine; life was amazing. That Christmas Eve we found out in front of friends and family that we were expecting a girl! We couldn't have been happier.

Around the same time as all of our joyous news, my boss became ill. Unsure as to when or if she would return, the owners of the company took a more active role. As the months went by, we found out that my boss would not be returning to work because of her illness. The company and the job started to change. What was once a 40 hour a week job became a 50 to 60 hour a week job. The morale of the company changed as well, and it was no longer a fun place to work. It became stressful. The expectations and priorities of the company seemed to change every day. It became difficult to keep my managers motivated, which in turn affected the mood of the stores. Employee problems began to arise and customer service started to decrease. It seemed everyone was having a difficult time with the shifts being made in the company. I did my best to encourage my managers to remain positive and help them push through the changes, and I decided to work up until I went into labor so I could be there for my team.

On a beautiful spring day, I delivered the most gorgeous baby girl at six in the morning. I spent three full weeks at home with her before I begged my doctor to approve me to return to work before the recommended six-week leave. At the time, I felt that the best thing for my family was to be sure my job was running smoothly. I felt I had to bring home the paychecks to support them. Therefore, my job came first. I poured all of my energy into my career only to get the news a month later that I was being laid off.

I was crushed, stunned, and devastated. Sad, angry, confused, and let down. I couldn't believe what had happened to me and to my family. I gave this company my all for seven years, had put them before my children, and for what? To be betrayed, to have them turn their back on me. I had just had a baby, and now I had no job and a household to support. I couldn't understand why I was the one being laid off; I was good at my job and made the company money. I couldn't help but wonder what I did and how I failed.

In an instant, everything that I defined myself as for years was gone. I no longer knew who I was or what I stood for. Worst of all, I felt like a failure and that I had let my family and co-workers down. I didn't just lose my job. I lost my confidence and my pride as well. I didn't know how we were going to pay the bills or buy groceries. Everything seemed to be crashing down around me, and I started to doubt my abilities and myself.

I applied to countless job listings and went on a handful of interviews, only to be denied by all of them. My self-worth continued plummeting. I got my real estate license in hopes of being able to design my life, take control of my destiny, and spend more time with my family. After a year of hustling and working 60 hours a week trying to make it in the industry with little money coming in and credit card debt piling up, my husband and I had to make a decision. We couldn't afford to keep our nanny and pay our bills, so that's the moment I became a stay-at-home mom, which was a huge adjustment for me.

Going from interacting with adults all day and contributing financially to our family to little to no adult interaction and making no money at all turned out to eat away at my self-worth more and more. I was unable to see the blessing that was right in front of me. Over the next year and a half, I tried multiple avenues of working from home to feel like I was contributing to the needs of the house. I needed to stay busy and make money to feel worthy, to feel important.

I didn't really make much money from these experiences, but I did become rich. Throughout my journey I met amazing people who helped me see that I was more than just a paycheck and a status. I started to dive into personal development books and follow people on social media that had a positive message and spoke of gratitude, self-love, the law of attraction, and empowerment from within. I began building up my confidence again and trust in my abilities after realizing that self-worth is not defined by how much money you make or your job status but by what you give to others and the positive impact you have on the people around you.

Your worth is determined by how you feel about yourself, not by the actions of others. My experience also brought me closer to my family. When I had baby number 5, it was the first of my children that I experienced EVERY milestone in the first year with. I watched him learn to crawl, walk, and climb. I introduced him to solids and watched him grow from an infant to the energetic toddler he is today. I don't believe in regrets and I know that everything in my past has pointed me to today. So I don't regret working during my other children's early years, but I am eternally grateful that I was able to experience it all with baby number 5 and that I will have the same opportunity with baby number 6, who I am pregnant with as I write this.

I have learned some valuable lessons since I was laid off three years ago: You are the only person who determines your value. Money, although nice, does not define you and make you who you are. I have learned that even in the darkest moments I have so much to be grateful for and when I focus on those things I am able to get through any darkness that is put in my path. And most of all, I have learned that I am strong, capable, intelligent, and I am a confident and beautiful woman.

LIFE LESSON:

You define who you are, no one else does. Don't let yourself forget that you are amazing.

Rebirth

by Nia M. Spence

**I believe in the proverbial saying that the way that
we talk to our children becomes their inner voice.**

GIFT:
SELF-LOVE

How we speak, see, and feel about our children is picked
up by them through their own powerful perception. It
is my belief that self-love or the lack thereof begins in
infancy and continues on throughout adulthood.

Growing up, I was an independent thinker. I loved
to read, write, climb trees and more. My household however, was somewhat strict and oppressive. I often felt I
couldn't be my true self. If I did, some "predator," my
mother led me to believe, would see the beauty in my
personality and try to hurt me as her step-father had hurt
her. In the name of protection, my mother's childhood
abuse stories were discussed constantly in our home

saturating my early childhood environment until I saw myself through her experiences and not my own. By the time I was a young adult, I was a basket case not knowing who to trust or how to relax with a lover. Over time I began to internalize myself as a victim unworthy of true parental love or a healthy sexual relationship with another.

Admittedly, it wasn't until I was 34 years old that I would be faced with a life or death situation that would serve as the catalyst for me to free myself from my mother's painful past and reclaim my own identity. Self-love and what it would mean to me was about to change forever.

In comes Natasha, a woman I would see often on my train ride to work. One day Natasha shared with me how she had been trying to get pregnant. As she talked, I discerned that like me, she didn't really feel worthy to have children. She felt like it just wasn't meant for her to have a family. I could defiantly relate. I was 33 years old and childless, yet the proud auntie of 29 nieces and nephews born to my five siblings. Ten of those children belonged to just one sister and another eight belonged to another. With two or more children belonging to each sibling compared to my ZERO, it was easy for me to feel like something was "wrong" with me.

Natasha, on the other hand, had medical proof that something was wrong with her. Turns out she had scar tissue around her ovaries that was interfering with conception. I tried to get her to see how the scar tissue was a possible emotional scarring linked to her childhood and that her ovaries could represent her mother. Her repressed feelings about her mother and the sexual abuse she experienced as a child were somehow blocking her ability to conceive. I understood these kinds of "mommy issues" very well and I wanted to help. I offered to write Natasha a future-based letter. In the letter she would already be pregnant and forgiving. "Dear mom, I am sooo super excited. We're having a baby! I'm going to be a mom! I'm seven months pregnant. My stomach is so big! I love this feeling. Now I know how you must have felt when you were carrying me...."

Before I could finish the letter, I found myself crying big, fat, sloppy tears of forgiveness. I cried for Natasha, I cried for me, and for every person that was still caught up in somebody else's nightmare fighting to break free. Exhausted, the next day, I called out of work and went to the doctors. I felt fatigued. I had no idea that one train ride and a urine test later, I would be hearing the most beautiful two words ever –YOU'RE PREGNANT! I was floored! This was a dream come true! Finally, at 33 years old I could take my place amongst the Great Mothers of the world. It felt great! I felt worthy. Within weeks Natasha had some good news of her own. She was also pregnant.

Moving on, I took good care of myself during my pregnancy. I ate healthy, danced a lot and spoke my daily affirmations aloud. I felt powerful and sexy. My skin was glowing and my hair grew longer. My sense of self that I carefully rebuilt out of the ashes of my childhood felt stronger. Every once in a while I would feel those lingering feelings of unworthiness creep up. It was like finally being pregnant was just too good to be true. After a while, my ingrained feelings of unworthiness eventually took over. I began to see myself and my unborn child through my old eyes. I feared my child would be born crippled or deformed. I wanted my mother to help ease my fears by participating in my pregnancy more, but she and my closest sister was nowhere to be found. By March 9th, I was 24 days overdue and my baby wasn't showing any signs of coming. My midwife was concerned. When she checked the baby's heart rate it had dropped.

We rushed to the hospital. On the way there I mentally prepared myself to have an optional cesarean. I already knew I would not be able to go through with a vaginal birth because my thoughts of pushing my baby out was very distorted. I didn't know how to relax and trust my body. I didn't even trust the people in the room. All kinds of damaging self-images kept popping up in my mind. I tried to shut them out, but I was too angry and hurt that my mother and favorite sister wasn't there. I begged for the cesarean to avoid going further. After the max amount of drugs administered and hours of not dilating past three centimeters, they eventually agreed to the surgery. Finally, I could get some rest. After my son was born I received devastating news. I had a Bandl's ring, a rare pathological retraction ring that happens one out of every 500 or so childbearing women. Instead of dilating I had begun to retract. Some women with a Bandl's ring give birth to babies that are stillborn. Turns out I had gotten the cesarean just in time before this very thick muscle formed a ring around my uterus separating the upper and lower segments until one of them, like a balloon, would eventually bust. WOW! So that was the depths of my unworthiness, I thought to myself as I deciphered the doctor's message.

Laying there on that operating table I had to make an important decision. Only I knew the value and symbolic meaning behind my ordeal. If I wanted to be a great mother, I would have to tend to my inner feelings of self-hate, or I could pass those feelings on to my child as my mother did to me. Symbolically the thick muscle the surgeons had to cut through just to get to my baby was the physical manifestation of the wounded self that had grown within me threatening the life of my own child before he was even born.

Ironically, after the surgery one of the surgeons mentioned that I would never be able to have a vaginal birth because of how deep and where they had to cut me. The spiritual translation: I MUST get this self-hate OUT of my emotional body if I want to raise emotionally healthy children. I decided I was going to have to truly love myself into wellness. Love myself into effective parenting. Love myself into my ideal birthing experience. Love myself for ME. All that crap I grew up believing about myself, I had to leave on the operating table. I chose life. I chose my son. I chose me. One day, after a few weeks of being home with my son lying in bed staring lovingly at each other, his eyes fully opened. I noticed for the first time a set of beautiful green eyes staring back at me. My son was the ONLY grandchild, out of 30, born with my late father's eye color and his name. Talk about feeling blessed. I felt like I hit the jackpot in baby heaven. To this day my son continues to amaze me with his beauty, intelligence and calm demeanor.

LIFE LESSON:

At times I ask myself what I did to deserve such a blessing. Then I ask myself why not me? I too am worthy. I too am deserved. God loves me too. We all owe it to ourselves to love ourselves as our self. Whenever an old wound tries to reassert itself through self-doubt or any of its emotional affiliates, calmly and confidently reaffirm to yourself what you know to be true. You are a WHOLE person, not a quarter or a half. You are worthy. Every day wake up appreciative of the self that only YOU can define. Today, I can proudly say that I am a generational curse breaker. The buck stops here.

Accepting My Own Beauty

by SharRon Jamison

I believe that all women are beautiful!

I have finally accepted that I'm beautiful. Understanding my beauty was not an easy task. Growing up where my blackness, kinky hair, thick lips and thick thighs were ridiculed, devalued, and caricaturized made it difficult for me to see my beauty. How could I even think I was attractive when black women were the subjects of disparaging remarks, vulgar statements, and pejorative comments that cultivated my self-hatred? How could I even consider my beauty when racism, sexism, classism, and being less-of-everything-ism stripped me of my ability to see myself, love myself, and love others who looked like me? How could I, a black girl, shaped and programmed to be and to feel inferior, inadequate, inaudible, and invisible even feel that being pretty was within my reach? How could I feel attractive when I was constantly referred to as an ape, monkey, buffalo, rhino, dog, and a cow? How could I understand how to love myself in the midst of such historical hatred, verbal violence, incessant toxicity, and societal-accepted negativity? How could I identify or even cultivate my beauty or my understanding of beauty in such a cesspool of perversion and degradation? How could an impressionable little girl, me, with limited understanding of the world think that I was beautiful? How?

The truth is that many little girls who looked like me didn't think that they were beautiful; they had been taught to devalue and discount themselves. They internalized and unknowingly carried those childhood messages of not being enough into adulthood. Those messages became their guides and templates for functioning in the world; for them, those negative messages were true.

And so, beautiful girls-turned-women now dim and, in many ways, extinguish their own light, downsize their goals, and lower their expectations. They embrace limits and lack because they believe that their lives either don't matter or matter less than their white, male counterparts. They don't love themselves, so they innocently choose people, places, and situations that validate their sense of worthlessness and nothingness. They were and still are beautiful, but they don't know it. They are adored, but they don't accept it.

How do I know that many women live in self-loathing? Because for years, I didn't like myself. I felt trapped by my own internalized self-hatred, and I secretly compared, competed, and conspired against my beautiful sisters. I secretly resented those who had the courage to love themselves and to live unapologetically in their truth. How dare they walk in their power when I felt as if I had crawl in defeat? How dare they speak boldly when I felt forced to whisper or to be silent? How dare they make their own rules when I felt confined and minimized by people and beliefs that imprisoned me? How dare these powerful women establish standards of engagement when I was not confident enough to erect my own emotional boundaries to protect my own heart, health, finances and spirit? How dare they feel radiant and exude vitality when I felt dull, bland, and lethargic? How dare they take care of their bodies when I felt uncomfortable, fat, and flappy? How dare they abandon faith traditions that spiritually disenfranchised them when I felt too scared to question my thoughts about God? How dare they be what I could not be, was too scared to be, didn't know how to be, and was not free enough to be? How dare they leave me in my brokenness while they enjoyed their lives?

In my early twenties, I bemoaned and blamed other women because I didn't understand that what I so deeply wanted was something that I had to give myself: self-love. I had to love and liberate myself from ways of functioning in the world that belittled me and prevented me from fully showing up in my power, passion, and purpose. I had to be my own rescue from beliefs and behaviors that failed to honor me. I had to analyze my life to identify why I consistently sabotaged my personal and professional dreams. I also had to stop choosing people who I perceived as less powerful to prop up my fragile façade and support my flimsy self-esteem.

I had to transform me; I could not sit on the sidelines of my life and wait for me to learn how to love me. I had to <u>decide</u> to love me, even if I had to make the same choice daily, minute by minute. If I wanted to be more comfortable, more secure, and vulnerable, I had to love me. And learning to love myself was not an easy journey. I failed tons of times and failed miserably. I had to deconstruct some of the childhood lessons that were entrenched in my psyche so that I could gain greater self-awareness, self-worth, and self-mastery. I had to accept responsibility to expose and analyze the bad fruit in my life to unearth the root of my self-loathing. It was my responsibility to do me, be me, understand me, speak for me, and most importantly, love me. I had abdicated that responsibility to others, who did not have my best interest at heart, for far too long. I had to admit the truth: I was the person limiting my life; it was ME.

The journey to self-love took a few years, but I took my time. I didn't want to replace self-hate with another mask or another lie. I didn't want to be a puppet and do what society considered, qualified, or promoted as self-love. I didn't want to parrot empty mantras, affirmations, and platitudes to shift my alignment. I wanted to learn me, unlearn me, and relearn me so that I could be fully ME, whatever that meant. I wanted to love myself in a way that resonated with my soul.

My journey illuminated things about me that I didn't know. For example, I learned that I was resilient in the face of adversity. I was adaptable in the midst of swift transitions. Creative in the midst of ambiguity. An implementer and executor. I was a sister who got things done. Hurray for me! I learned that my body was strong and responded to discipline and exercise. I learned that God was not a person in heaven, but a spirit that resided everywhere, even in my soul. I learned that I was different and that the years of being labeled a misfit was how others acknowledged my uniqueness. It is surprising what you can learn about yourself when you move out of your comfort zone, fear zone, or any other zone that confines you. I am amazing. Makes me wonder why I was tripping.

When I reflect on those developing years, I feel triumphant. I feel joyful and blessed. Radiant and beautiful! I am proud that the girl who was so convinced that she was ugly, stupid, worthless, and awkward is now helping other women understand their worth. I feel proud that those hurtful messages that made me a prisoner of pain and trapped me in dysfunction is now a distant memory. I feel so proud that the young woman who felt *less than* now realizes that she is *more than* capable of making meaningful contributions to society. I feel proud that I can now celebrate other women and learn from them, champion them, advocate for them, and accept the same care in return.

Women are beautiful, not because society acknowledges or celebrates their beauty, but because they are. Women are divinely created masterpieces: feminine and masculine, strong and fragile, independent and interdependent, leaders and followers. Women are amazing; they are bold, brilliant, and beautiful! Yes, women are beautiful because they are not limited by images portrayed in the media, not confined by norms endorsed by their culture and not restricted by labels enforced by society. Women are beautiful in ways that defy explanation and challenge convention. We women, all of us, are beautiful.

It's true. You can never love yourself without understanding the beliefs that kept you trapped, fearful, and defeated. You can never love yourself if you fail to appreciate that you are uniquely made, divinely-inspired, and specifically equipped to answer your unique call. You can never love yourself without making a decision to, as everything starts with a choice. But most of all, you can never love someone else beyond your ability to love yourself. You must love YOURSELF first—the good, the bad, the indifferent, the contradictory, the less-than-stellar, the highs, the lows, the unique, the strong, the fragile.... YOU! From out of the well of self-love flows peace, abundance, and joy.

LIFE LESSON:

You are beautiful just as you are. So, love yourself. You deserve the best love in the world, and that loves resides in you, beautiful woman!

Blessings to you always!

Claim All That Is Yours

by Tepsii

I believe that those who have endured deep pain can become our greatest guides when it comes to enjoying the present moment, being grateful for what we have, and moving into the future with love.

GIFT:
GRATITUDE

"I didn't ask you to have me! You made this choice, not me."

Have you?

Those are the words of a defiant, spoiled little brat born with privilege oozing out of her ears and expectations of obligations owed to her a mile long. She is me. The same she who didn't know better—who watched too many teenage angst movies and borrowed her vocabulary and was trying to act grown by talking back and acting sassy, forgetting that, unlike the other mothers, hers was a powerful African matriarch at the helm of their household and had zero chill when it came to disrespect.

My mother demanded excellence in everything from personal hygiene to proper speech and academics. Funny enough, she extended these expectations to my friends who were expected to act like ladies, greet her appropriately on the phone and in person or risk being refused entry in our home. (I laugh now, but back then I used to cringe.)

At 14, with limited life experience and zero street sense, how could I have known that would be the last argument I'd ever have with my mom? How could I have known that I'd come back from a 7 a.m. workout and walk through the door on a bright and frosty Saturday morning to find my dad crying for the first time ever. How could I have known that not even a month after celebrating the quintessential immigrant milestone of moving into our big American dream home, my mom would be dead?

When I walked in on my dad, I instinctively and intuitively knew. But I asked anyway. Voice cracking, knees wobbling, eyes already watering, I already knew. But I wanted to hear, just for confirmation. "What happened to my mom?" I asked. The words I heard back were deafening. They rang through my ears for years to come.

"She's dead," he said. Nothing more. Nothing less. He was in shock himself, I guess. My life and the parts of hers that I'd witnessed or been told about flashed before my eyes. As the tears raced one another down my cheek, I saw flashes of red, pink, yellow, and orange. After the incident, a huge, painful lump that made it hard to swallow immediately grew in my throat (that lump was there for over a year).

My reaction? I screamed and yelled. Loud. A combo of no and why and nooooooo, not me. Then I ran, feet pounding against the brand-spanking new wood floor all the way to our study. I locked the door, threw myself on the cushy, white carpet, and continued crying until I lost track of time and exhausted myself.

It was early afternoon when I went into the study and late into the night when I finally emerged. Vocal chords shredded, eyes swollen, spirit disheveled. Even then, I only came up for air because I had to go to the bathroom. You see, I knew right then that my life was about to change—big time. Until then, I'd been shielded from hardships and the struggles of what it actually meant to be an alien, an immigrant, a foreigner in America. I'd lived comfortably as my parents jumped through the logistical hoops on my behalf.

√ Education, including multiple degrees, while juggling work at night

√ Visas, Green cards, citizenship

√ The picket-fence, cars, and trappings

As soon as it seemed that we had it all, it was repossessed in one freaky-and-foul fell swoop.

A car accident. Rain. A tollgate. Head injury. She never woke up.

That's all I know. Afraid to further traumatize the storytellers and afraid to hear the truth, I've never asked for more details. And I'm not sure I'll ever ask for more about how she died. Even without knowing the details, my imagination's done all the work. I saw the car, a big '90s model Mercedes C-Class smashed beyond recognition. That image informs me and gives me more than I need to know and puts thoughts in my mind that I wish I could unsee.

Losing my mom was the hardest thing I've ever experienced. Yes, she was strict and had high standards for me and the others in her life. On the other hand, though, I've yet to meet anyone who has the capacity to love that she did. She loved people so hard that they learned how to love themselves. A person with that kind of love is rare. As soon as we lost her, I knew that I had options. I could give up, go into depression, and forget about life. Or I could LIVE! I could live, even with the understanding that everything could be taken away the blink of an eye. I could live through those hard moments when pain prevailed. I could live, fill myself with gratitude, and eventually find happiness again.

I chose life. To experience life in full color and to love and laugh, no matter what. In those moments, I was guided by my faith and carried by something much bigger than me. A voice in my head told me that my mom, with her quiet strength and high expectations, would never have settled for less from me! By going through that experience at such a young age, I realized no one has immunity when it comes to experiencing life-altering events—not even the hardest-working duo, my parents, who had finally checked off all the boxes and acquired all the status symbols as if to say, "You see, we do belong here, America. Will you call us yours?"

Since then I've almost never held back. I've hardly waited on doing or being who I wanted to be. I've never let my dreams die, even after going through a physically abusive marriage, getting an abortion, experiencing rape, harassment, and pain beyond measure. The years after losing my mom were tough. My soul was craving a sense of home, so I put myself through a lot of unsavory experiences and allowed people to abuse me for almost 10 years after she died because I thought it was better to have people around to fill a deep void than to be alone. My dad was grieving. He was with my mom since they were teenagers. They were raised together and their parents were friends before they were born. My maternal and paternal grandfathers worked together as teachers and were even roommates at one time. My dad lost his father at age 7 in a car accident, so when my mom was killed in a similar way, it broke his heart and took quite some time to recover.

I'm grateful for those experiences. I got myself into them, and then I rescued myself and got myself out of each and every one of them. Whenever I get too comfortable and think *Oh, no. I'll wait and do that tomorrow or next year*, I remember my mom.

Lufuno Maumela Tshikororo. She never waited for tomorrow, she loved fiercely and lived as if every day was her last. She must have had a sense of knowing, because she packed a ton in her 35 years. Me and my cousin, Mpho, whom she adopted; years of marriage to her loving man; then two master's degrees and a Ph.D. in just four years. On top of that she traveled, enjoyed friendships, nurtured relationships with her parents, brothers, and extended family. She cultivated a successful career, experienced adventure, and infused humor into it all.

With her last breath she did not simply die. She left me with love and a legacy that lives on. No one who meets me can feel sad for me or even pity because, the truth is, my childhood was filled with love. And in my present life, I experience love in all forms from my husband, my three girls, my dad, grandparents, aunts, uncles, and at least five surrogate moms. My mom had such amazing relationships with her friends and coworkers that they continue pouring love into me, even though it's been almost 20 years since we said goodbye to her.

The real lesson I've gotten out of the experiences I've been through is that life can be short, but it's up to you to make it sweet. At the end of the day you'll regret more of what you didn't do than what you did do.

I encourage you to:

- Pay tribute to your parents for all they did and forgive them for all they didn't do.

- Send love to all of the people in your life, whether they do good by you or not.

- Be kind to yourself, love yourself, and work on yourself before you start worrying about anyone else.

- Develop a spiritual practice that will take you through the ups and downs of life.

- Infuse gratitude into all aspects of your life, as gratitude attracts abundance. You deserve every last thing you want in this world, and you'll get it by being grateful.

LIFE LESSON:

I know that you have dealt with your own burdens, your own trials, and your own tribulations in this life. You may be reading this because you feel a desire for something bigger and greater in your life. Never let that dream go. Go after your dreams. Fight fiercely to claim all that's yours. Simply because you deserve it, and damn it you're worth it. So don't give up, okay? Pinky-promise me that you'll keep going!

Love,
Tepsii

About the Authors

Kim Coles

Kim Coles is a beloved actress, comedian, and speaker, most known for her role as an original cast member on the sketch comedy, *In Living Color*, and as the loveable Synclaire on the long-running hit Fox series, *Living Single*. In 1998, she became a published author with *I'm Free, but It'll Cost You*, a hilarious guide for frustrated women in the dating scene.

Soon after *Living Single* was cancelled, Kim waded into a deep depression. As her weight increased, her funds decreased. Having lost sight of her self-worth and self-esteem, her survival required a drastic change of mind. The first step was finding a therapist, and the tools gained through therapy flipped her perspective and her life right-side up again. She realized that while she has a phenomenal gift of performance, she also has a spiritual calling to help women access their own gifts, share them with others, and enjoy a more fulfilled life.

Kim has since regained control of her life, married her soulmate, starred in several films and television shows, hosted the BET game show *Pay It Off* and the inaugural Indie Author Legacy Awards for independent authors, and published *Open Your G.I.F.T.S*, a collaborative book for women in search of a deeper level of satisfaction in their lives.

Precious Bivings

Precious is a celebrated life and business coach, author, speaker, philanthropist, and risk taker who made a conscious decision to abandon all excuses and distractions in order to pursue her purpose of inspiring, empowering, and developing leaders to grow to their highest personal and professional level. Her success has allowed her to engage a unique following with a reach that spans 5,000 followers on multiple platforms. Her coaching practice and virtual community Surrender, Work, Live Coaching and Accountability allows Precious to continue growing and empowering leaders to manifest their dreams, kill their excuses, and serve in their true purpose and their authentic self with clarity in the highest capacity possible. To connect with Precious or learn more about her, visit www.preciousbivings.com or Facebook, Twitter and Instagram at Precious Bivings.

Heidi Dietrich

Heidi lives on the South Shore of Boston with her husband and three children. She is a Partner and the EVP of Strategy & Business Development for What Vibes Your Tribe Media; Editor of FT Pulse; a Thought Leadership Marketing Strategist; Content Creator; Media, PR, and Publishing Executive; a Writer for Thrive Global; and a Wellness Enthusiast for optimal Health, Wealth, Love & Happiness. Leading with gratitude, Heidi's greatest gifts are her intuition, optimism, and her ability to see the good in every situation—making lemonade from lemons. Heidi is the host of the Podcast, *The Diet Rich Life - Life Mastery for Health, Wealth, Love, and Happiness*; co-host of the podcast "What Vibes Your Tribe"; and author of the 2017 title, *Joseph's Miracle*.

To learn more visit www.whatvibesyourtribe.com
or contact Heidi at Heidi@wvytmedia.com

Kathleen Lynch

Kathleen T. Lynch's first book entitled *Overcoming Fear of Madness* will be released in 2017. Kathleen writes about her passions, health and wellness, with special emphasis on mental health. Kathleen lives and works in the north suburbs of Chicago and is active in support of groups like NAMI, American Heart Association, Making Strides for Breast Cancer, and Alzheimer's Association. She loves to walk and participates in many 5ks in support of these charities. Contact Kathleen at @popcornt on Twitter, @1kinddiva on Instagram, and @KathleenLynch1Focus on Facebook.

Lee Tkachuk

Lee Tkachuk is a serial entrepreneur and founder of Keystrokes Transcription Service, Ellipsys, SpeechCheck, Girly-Girls Know Sports, and Lee Tkachuk – Limitless! She is a professional speaker, a born entertainer, knowledgeable teacher, and avid Chicago sports fan. She and her husband, Jeff, live part of the year in the far west suburbs of Chicago and the rest of the year in South Florida, a short drive from their son, Jeffrey, who goes to school and lives in nearby Miami. With a passion for teaching others and a love for travel, you can find Lee speaking at conferences and meetings, coaching others on improving their presentations and speaking skills, and sharing her knowledge while helping fellow entrepreneurs avoid the speed bumps, potholes, and brick walls that often come with starting and growing a business! Contact Lee by phone at (630) 385-7504 or via her websites at www.LeeTkachuk.com and www.GirlyGirlsKnowSports.com.

Ashley Ann

Ashley Jones of Ashley Ann's Events is a talented, award-winning wedding and event designer. She is equipped with a B.A. in Finance and an M.B.A. She is also an outstanding business woman excelling in social media, lead generations, lead magnets, funnels, and return paths. Known for her creative and unusual event ideas and producing large scale events, she has become one of the most sought after event designers in the South.

In the business world, Ashley is known for getting results and simplifying social media and CVO so that her clients achieve desired outcomes. She pays exquisite attention to every last detail in the boardroom and in the ballroom. Ashley's bright personality and calm demeanor help her clients relax as she creates one-of-a-kind atmospheres. For more information, visit: www.AshleyAnnSpeaks.com or Facebook.com/ashleyannevents

Melanie Anderson

Born and raised in Memphis, TN, Melanie Anderson discovered her love for acting at a young age, but did not pursue her dreams right away. Instead, she became a teen mom at the age of sixteen and was diagnosed with Lupus in 2011. Initially, she thought this was her death sentence but eventually realized Lupus saved her by pushing her to follow her dreams of becoming an actress. Despite all her challenges, she earned a Bachelor's degree in Business Administration in 2012. The following year, Melanie stepped out on faith, relocating to Atlanta where she booked her first commercial and her first role in a TV series for BET, earning her first acting credit. Now she is an actress, inspirational speaker, co-author, and entrepreneur. Melanie is passionate about sharing her life experiences to inspire and encourage other women and teenagers, letting them know that it's never too late to follow your dreams. Twitter: @IAMMELANDERSON Website: IAMMELANIEANDERSON.COM

Shade Adu

Shadé Y. Adu is a personal brand strategist, international speaker, bestselling author, and founder of Savvy Solutions Consulting, LLC. Shade teaches high-achieving entrepreneurs how to leverage the power of social media and live streaming in order to build profitable brands and create digital products and services that change lives. Shadé has been featured in Hello Beautiful, Black Enterprise, The Huffington Post, The Network Journal, and the Rachel Ray Show. As a former international educator, she has traveled the world inspiring others to live their best lives and accept their greatness. Shadé has spoken at and facilitated numerous workshops in Kazakhstan, Ghana, as well as universities, high schools, and institutions throughout the United States. Follow her on social media @shadeyaabirago

Lakesha Williams

LaKesha L. Williams, acclaimed award-wining author and speaker, was born to Doris and Cleo Williams in Raleigh, North Carolina in 1983. To know LaKesha is to experience a calming spirit infused with gut-wrenching laughter at unexpected times. She has a passion for giving, which is demonstrated whole-heartedly through her founding of Born Overcomers, Inc., a non-profit organization and movement dedicated to spreading the belief that we were all born to overcome. She has authored six books and is also the owner of Ministry Motivators, a consulting firm with a primary focus on supporting individuals, businesses, and ministries. LaKesha, a proud virgin, is also an advocate of abstinence and purity. She currently resides in Southern Maryland and enjoys serving in the community and fellowshipping with her church family at Light of Glory Ministries, and watching movies and creating new memories with her family and friends. Website: www.lakeshalwilliams.com

Veleda Spellman

Veleda Spellman is the CEO of Positive Queens, actor, author, and motivational speaker. Positive Queens is a Facebook group that encompasses over 94,000 women nationwide. She mothers three sons, Justin, Steven, and Marcus, and grandmothers her first grandchild, Avianna. Born and raised in Riverhead N.Y under the Christian upbringing of her parents, William Spellman and Margaret Spellman, she is the sixth of eight children. After graduating high school, she furthered her education at Suffolk County Community College where she received her Associates of Arts degree. She later attended Stonybrook University where she studied politics and theater arts. Additionally, she has also acted in many television shows such as *Orange is the New Black, Law and Order*, and *Investigative Discovery Television* to name a few.

D. L. Jordan

D.L. Jordan is a native New Yorker who lives in Brooklyn with her husband, son, and daughter. She is the author and writer of *Living Life Like It's Golden* and *The Latter Years of My Life Shall Be the BEST Years of My Life*! Aside from her staffed position with Assembly member Pamela Harris, she likes networking and meeting new people and also enjoys reading, cooking, and the great outdoors. She graduated from TOURO/NYSCAS College with a Bachelor's degree in Liberal Arts and Sciences and a Masters in Science of Psychology from the University of Phoenix. She is currently working on her next book, a children's series, and a book of poetry. You can visit and connect with her at DlJordan4@aol.com and on Facebook and Twitter @dljordan4

Ca Bap

Ca Bap lives by the mantra "Live your life to the fullest." Grounded in faith, she views her spirituality as a direct gateway to the voice within. Ca Bap retired as the second African-American woman locomotive engineer in the history of the company for which she worked. She is an advocate for living fearlessly and has hosted several women's groups to motivate women to face their fears and step out of their comfort zone. Ca Bap loves traveling and exploring other cultures, and she is constantly developing her talents, gifts, and interests. Ca Bap found a natural way to treat her skin as a result of having discoid lupus, using FAB 222 Body Butter Crème, created by her team of shea chefs. Ca Bap's famous saying is: Dream, Create, Live, Love, and Laugh! Connect with Ca Bap on Facebook: Fab222BodyButterCreme and Twitter: BeFab222

Ms. Candy Blog

Ms. Candy Blog is "where candy is always in vogue." It's a personality driven vlog with a focus on candy as it translates to fashion and beauty. With a degree in English, two in theatre, and a background in corporate training, instructional design and community management, Ms. Candy Blog has worked for Google/YouTube, Yahoo!, J.P. Morgan, and Citysearch. She has partnered with top brands such as Hershey's, Lindt, HSN, Epix, It'Sugar, Sour Patch Kids, Just Born (Peeps/Mike & Ike), Jelly Belly, and more. Her award-nominated YouTube channel is part of the World of Wonder network. Additionally, she was awarded a contract with Periscope's first talent network, Lifestream Productions and placed on three top Periscope lists after her first week livestreaming. Ms. Candy Blog is also proud to be part of Revry, the first LGBTQ streaming platform for television. Connect with her on social media @mscandyblog and at www.mscandyblog.com

April L Butcher

April L Butcher is a Branding Agent, Founder of PERIUNION, and Huffington Post Contributor. April Butcher is a Solutions Sorceress, using her acquired knowledge and wisdom to connect people to resources so solutions are made and that magic can happen. In a world that is constantly moving, it is imperative to stay connected. Last year, April found herself confused, overwhelmed, and disconnected with her social media brand. In March of 2016, she hosted her first LIVE event, PERIUNION, to teach others how to connect the dots between business and social media to gain clarity. The event was a huge success with over 75 attendees and six major sponsors. She will be launching her second annual event in March 2017. April is also a YouTube vlogger who shares her authenticity and transparency. Connect with her further at www.aprilbutcher.com or Twitter: AprilLButcher

Tanisha Mackin

Award-winning author Tanisha D. Mackin is a cancer survivor, bestselling author, writing coach, and creator of the Destiny Collection, a line of sassy and fun stationery designed to inspire you. She is also the founder of the Mackin Project, a non-profit organization that provides bereavement coaching, encouragement, and care packages to those who've lost a spouse or parent to violence. Tanisha used her tragedies to motivate others through their pain. When asked what inspires her, Tanisha looks no further than her two beautiful children. She's a recipient of the 2013 Utopian Euphoria Making a Difference 2016 Metro Phenomenal Women, 2016 Black Women Are Award for survivorship, the 2016 IALA award for Memoir of the Year, and the 2016 Rising Star award. Her experiences and opportunities led her to write books, write for magazines, and appear on radio shows, television interviews, as well as newspaper articles.

Faye Thompson

Faye Thompson is an Ohio native who calls New York home. She has been writing almost all her life. Her drama-drenched gems with purpose are designed to reconnect us with our first love—the God who loved us first. A retired federal government employee, Faye is busy at work on her fifth romantic gem, *Mocha Madness*, a love story that addresses mental illness and is scheduled to be released in spring 2017. A portion of the book's proceeds will be donated to the National Alliance on Mental Illness (nami.org). Visit her website www.dontsitonyourfabulous.com to purchase her "Don't Sit on Your Fabulous" T-shirts and mugs, and to subscribe to her blog. Speaking engagements, interviews, and book signings can be scheduled via author@fayethompson.com or through Facebook: FayeThompsonnow.

LaKita Stewart-Thompson

LaKita Stewart-Thompson is a woman of faith, mother, entrepreneur, advocate, philanthropist, writer, and two-time best-selling author. With great passion, Lakita has helped many women discover their pain and define their life's purpose. Inspired by her passion to change lives, LaKita focuses on ways to empower, educate, and encourage women and girls who experience brokenness. Through the struggles of depression, abuse, divorce, and other life hardships, Ms. Thompson established several platforms for women to include her signature program, The I Am HerStory Movement, purposed to equip women with the confidence to share their stories and change lives through words. As a result, over 80 women have become successful authors and advocates in their specific areas, impacting women all over the world with their testimonies from pain to purpose. LaKita currently resides in Maryland, where she enjoys writing, traveling, and spending time with her amazing daughter Destinee, the sunshine of her life!

Jennifer Hill

Jennifer Hill is a transformational coach and the founder of HeadTurners.Org, a health and wellness organization encouraging women to embrace the most powerful, confident and uniquely beautiful version of themselves by coaching them through a series of self-care techniques. She is a certified fitness professional and Behavior Change Specialist. A former sponsored athlete and brand ambassador, Jennifer has been featured in *Weight Watcher's* Magazine, *The Chicago Sun-Times*, and appears as a guest writer for NiaMagazine. com. For more information, go to www.HeadTurners.Org or contact info@HeadTurners.Org.

Sherie Wells

Sherie is a wife and a mother to six children, as well as an online entrepreneur. Her business is focused on instilling a positive mindset, confidence, and a can-do attitude in children of all ages so they may carry these traits with them into adulthood. Sherie also believes in helping parents encourage their children's entrepreneurial spirit while adopting habits for success and the skills necessary to confidently share their stories, products, and business with the world at an early age. Engaging children in these behaviors, she asserts, will steer them on the path to success as adults and help give them the freedom to design their own lives. For more information, visit: SherieWells.com

Nia Spence

Nia Spence is a first-time mom, blogger, and public speaker. She is the founder and CEO of SpenceSpeaks Publications LLC., a digital publishing company that specializes in Law of Attraction based material. She is a widely sought after public speaker and virtual coach/consultant within the Law of Attraction community. Her customized course(s): *21 days to Talk Yourself into ANYTHING* can be found on her website www.spence-speakspublications.com. For a daily dose of healthy vortex living and inspiration, please visit her blog: vortex-living.com, follow her on: Instagram@ niaspencespeaks and Facebook.com/YourVortexCoach, or email her at niaspence@vortexliving.com

SharRon Jamison

MBA Inspirational Speaker, minister, life strategist, entrepreneur, and author, SharRon Jamison is the Founder/CEO of The Jamison Group, a leadership, relationship and empowerment training company. SharRon earned a B.A. degree from Hampton University, an MBA from Nova Southeastern University, and is currently pursuing her M.Div. degree at the Interdenominational Theological Center. SharRon is a passionate speaker, seasoned facilitator, an empathetic life coach, a business professional, a licensed minister, a proud mother, and the author of three books: *I Can Depend on Me, I Have Learned a Few Things* and *The Strength of My Soul: Stories of Sisterhood, Triumph and Inspiration.* She is also a contributing author in three upcoming anthologies. Her newest book, *50 Choices to a Fulfilling Life* is scheduled for release in early 2017. You can connect with SharRon on all social media platforms under her name. Visit SharRon Jamison at www.SharRonJamison.com

Tepsii

Tepsii is the creator of Sold Out + Booked Solid, her flagship online Business Incubator Program/Mastermind, and her signature Copywriting Course, The Write to Profit™. Tepsii has over 13 years of experience as a professional writer and works as a Soulful Copywriter and Business Coach with a degree in Public Communication. She was born with the gift of authentic expression and has written promotional materials that resulted in five- and six-figure program launches for clients. Since starting her business, she has amassed a following that includes over 16,000 fans, followers, and subscribers. Tepsii has worked with over 100 private clients and made six-figures within her first year in business. She is also the founder of the Copybesties Online Business Community, the one-stop shop for entrepreneurs who want to quickly and easily learn branding, write their own copy, and manage their own legal business affairs online. Connect with Tepsii at www.tepsii.com.

CREATING DISTINCTIVE BOOKS
WITH INTENTIONAL RESULTS

We're a collaborative group of creative masterminds
with a mission to produce high-quality books to position
you for monumental success in the marketplace.

Our professional team of writers, editors, designers,
and marketing strategists work closely together to ensure
that every detail of your book is a clear representation
of the message in your writing.

Want to know more?
Write to us at info@publishyourgift.com
or call (888) 949-6228

Discover great books, exclusive offers, and more at
www.PublishYourGift.com

Connect with us on social media

@publishyourgift

CPSIA information can be obtained
at www.ICGtesting.com
Printed in the USA
BVOW06s1143070617
486069BV00007B/16/P